"*Advent with St. Teresa of Calcutta* is the perfect prayer companion for my Advent journey. Heidi's anecdotes and interesting facts about St. Teresa, plus the inclusion of all three cycles of readings, complement the brief but inspiring reflections and daily prayers that make this a versatile book for the Advent season. Perfect for personal reflection or a family devotional."

—Maria Morera Johnson, author, *My Badass Book of Saints*

"Heidi Saxton's reflections lead us along a path of holiness as we walk daily with St. Teresa of Calcutta. This book helps us to journey through Advent and special feasts of the Christmas season as we deepen our love of Christ."

—Kathleen Egan, OSB, coauthor, *Suffering Into Joy:*
What Mother Teresa Teaches About True Joy

"In this beautifully written devotional, author and editor Heidi Hess Saxton gives us the life, writings, and prayers of St. Teresa of Calcutta to help us ready our hearts to welcome our Lord. The meditations, reflection questions, and applications on the daily liturgical readings draw us closer week by week to the coming of our Savior. I suggest that you let St. Teresa join your family around your Advent wreath and let her joyful spirit refresh you as you anticipate Christmas."

—Bert Ghezzi, author, *Voices of the Saints*

"Praying with Heidi Saxton's inspirational new book, *Advent With Saint Teresa of Calcutta,* is as intimate as a quiet chat with a treasured friend: spiritual and practical, intimate and wise. Saxton's honest storytelling and insightful commentary make this beautiful devotional the must-have of the Advent season."

—Lisa Mladnich, author, *True Radiance: Finding Grace in the Second Half of Life*

ADVENT
WITH
Saint
Teresa
OF CALCUTTA

Daily
Meditations

. . . .

Heidi Hess Saxton

FOREWORD BY
DONNA-MARIE COOPER O'BOYLE

servant
AN IMPRINT OF
FRANCISCAN MEDIA
Cincinnati, Ohio

Cover and book design by Mark Sullivan
Cover image © Corbis | Tim Graham

LIBRARY OF CONGRESS CATALOGING-IN-PUBLICATION DATA
Names: Saxton, Heidi Hess, author.
Title: Advent with St. Teresa of Calcutta : daily meditations / Heidi Hess Saxton ; foreword by Donna-Marie Cooper O'Boyle.
Description: Cincinnati : Servant, 2016. | Includes bibliographical references and index.
Identifiers: LCCN 2016025671 | ISBN 9781632531346 (trade paper : alk. paper)
Subjects: LCSH: Advent—Meditations. | Christmas—Meditations. | Teresa, Mother, 1910-1997.
Classification: LCC BV40 .S293 2016 | DDC 242/.33—dc23
LC record available at https://lccn.loc.gov/2016025671

ISBN 978-1-63253-134-6

Copyright ©2016, Franciscan Media. All rights reserved.
Published by Servant
an imprint of Franciscan Media
28 W. Liberty St.
Cincinnati, OH 45202
www.FranciscanMedia.org

Printed in the United States of America.
Printed on acid-free paper.
16 17 18 19 20   5 4 3 2 1

Contents

Feast Days and Other Special Days
during Advent and Christmas | *111*

Notes | *121*

Foreword
DONNA-MARIE COOPER O'BOYLE

The very first time I caught a glimpse of Mother Teresa was when she walked quietly past me in the chapel just before Mass began. My heart soared to see her. She was so small in stature, but I knew without a doubt that she was a powerhouse of faith, hope, and love. I was visiting the Missionaries of Charity chapel with my family because the Sisters had invited us to their private Mass in Washington DC after we had spent some time with the patients in their Home of the Dying.

As I kept watch over my children and was trying to focus my heart on the Mass that was about to begin, I felt a strong holy presence come beside me. I quickly glanced to my left and there she was—the hero of the poorest of the poor walking quietly right past me in her bare feet! While I was certainly excited that we would be united in prayer together at holy Mass, I told myself to get my mind back on the Mass that would soon start—never mind the fact that a living saint was in my midst!

Mass was very beautifully celebrated in the modest chapel as earnest prayers from dozens of holy virgins' hearts ascended to God like wafting aromatic incense. I felt incredibly blessed that my family was in the presence of so many saints in the making—the priest, Mother Teresa, and all of the Missionaries of Charity Sisters. But, I was also keenly convinced that Mother Teresa was already quite saintly and that she had been ardently and wholeheartedly following God's holy will in her life in taking care of the poorest of the poor all around the world.

That morning, kneeling there on the hard, bare floor for Mass, I had no clue—not even a whisper of an inkling—that an unimaginable friendship between me, a suburban housewife, and a world-renowned missionary of the poor would soon unfold through nearly two dozen personal letters and more than a dozen additional face-to-face meetings.

After Mass, I was privileged with a beautiful and unforgettable conversation with that humble Nobel Peace Prize recipient as we stood together in the convent's foyer. Mother Teresa took the time to reach out to my family and gave us each a blessed Miraculous Medal along with her blessings. When we bid our good-byes, my children and I gave her warm hugs. She, in turn, hugged us back and asked for our prayers before parting our company.

Over the next ten years, I learned so much from Mother Teresa as I relished in family joys—bringing two more children into the world—as well as tried to navigate through some arduous and challenging times in my life. Mother Teresa's instructions to me always echoed in my heart. Her loving encouragement pushed me onward to strive to continue to put one foot in front of the other to walk in faith and to trust God with my life.

In time, I endeavored to pass on the blessings and wisdom that I received from that humble servant of the Lord through my writings and talks. Mother Teresa has so much to teach us. She emphasized that "Love begins at home." We absolutely need to take care of our families before running out to try and change the world. She said we should strive to find times of silence for prayer even in our noisy world. She encouraged us all to a life of prayer and holiness, saying, "Holiness is not the luxury of a few, but a simple duty for you and me." Mother Teresa made it quite clear that it was necessary for her to receive the broken bread of Jesus in the Eucharist every morning for strength to do her work in taking care of the broken bodies of the poor. Her simple yet powerful one-on-one approach of meeting each need that unfolded before her teaches us to do the same—to not lose opportunities to serve Jesus in others and to pray and trust God, asking Him to use us to bring others to Him.

Advent with St. Teresa of Calcutta: Daily Mediations is guaranteed to stir your heart to emulate St. Teresa of Calcutta's virtuous life. Take the time to pause, ponder, and pray during the grace-filled Advent season and strive to apply the beautiful lessons expressed in this book to your own life. With God's grace, and Mother Teresa's help, you can "make your life something beautiful for God," as this small, but spirited, saint was famous for saying.

Introduction

The season of Advent is like springtime in nature,
when everything is renewed
and so is fresh and healthy.
Advent is also meant to do this to us—
to refresh us and make us healthy,
to be able to receive Christ
in whatever form he may come to us.[1]

Clad like her spiritual daughters in a simple blue-and-white sari, this diminutive yet undeniably charismatic nun traveled to more than a hundred countries with a message of faith, hope, and unrelenting love. With humility, Mother Teresa, now St. Teresa of Calcutta, sought out the poorest and loneliest, those who endured both physical and spiritual poverty. In each of their faces she saw her beloved Spouse, "Jesus in distressing disguise."

Though she was "Mother" to thousands, she did not always feel the love and joy she espoused; rather, she chose it, and in so doing she embodied the kind of faith that speaks hope and courage to those who likewise struggle. For those who wander in darkness, St. Teresa of Calcutta is a true patron of joy yet to be discovered.

Born Agnes Gonxha Bojaxhiu on August 27, 1910, to a family of Albanian descent, she left her family at eighteen to become a novice in the

Sisters of Our Lady of Loreto, an Irish missionary order of nuns dedicated to educating children in India. In 1948, she received her "call within a call" to start her own order dedicated to tending the needs of the poorest and most marginalized of Calcutta. This represented no small sacrifice on her part, for she was a natural teacher. But in 1952 she and some of her former students opened their first home for the dying, and the following year the Missionaries of Charity opened their first orphanage.

For more than fifty years, Mother Teresa traveled the world in order to meet the needs of the physically and spiritually impoverished alike. She won the Nobel Peace Prize in 1979; in June 1997 she received the Congressional Medal of Honor. And yet, in her lifetime she garnered alternately great recognition and heavy criticism alike for her unflinching truths. Time and time again, she shed her particular brand of light on polarizing subjects, at once enticing the disillusioned and offending those determined to stumble on in darkness. They could argue with her views, but there was no denying the love with which she spoke—a heart completely and unrelentingly faithful to her beloved Spouse.

When she died on September 5, 1997, more than fifteen thousand attended her funeral. On October 19, 2003, she was beatified by her good friend Pope John Paul II. And yet, when her private letters were published in 2007 in *Mother Teresa: Come Be My Light,* the world caught a glimpse of a woman who had spent decades in the shadows, unable to feel God's presence. "If ever I become a saint—I will surely be one of 'darkness,'" she wrote. "I will continually be absent from Heaven—to light the light of those in darkness on earth."[2]

On September 4, 2016, this indefatigable handmaid of the Lord was declared a saint. Today her Missionaries of Charity, both the professed

Sisters and the more than 5000 members of the lay order, reach 740 homes in Calcutta and 145 centers around the world.[3]

This book captures this humble yet faith-filled spirit of this great lady of Calcutta. As you gather around the supper table each evening, light the Advent candles and remember the words of St. Teresa…and the self-giving love of the Savior who was also not afraid to humble himself, to be born in that poor little stable in Bethlehem.

As you pray, consider what to offer the Lord as a gift to him during this Christmas season. Reflect upon the words of St. Teresa, and consider how you might love more deeply, surrender more completely, and let go of the things you do not need so there is more room to receive from the Lord all he wishes for you to have.

There can never be too much love; there is never a time when love is inappropriate, for love is what God *is*, and love constitutes the very life of heaven. Mind you, in heaven there is no need for faith, and hope fades away. But in that supremely holy place, love remains in all of its infinite intensity and radicality. Mother Teresa's way of life, accordingly, is an icon of the love that will obtain in heaven, when we are drawn utterly into the very life of God.[4]

—Bishop Robert Barron

How to Use This Book

Because the number of days in Advent vary from year to year, this booklet includes twenty-eight daily meditations, seven for each of the four weeks of Advent (not all of them may be needed in a given year, depending on what date Christmas falls).

The readings for the fourth week of Advent are based on the "O Antiphons," which are traditionally read from December 17 through December 23. (You may need to omit some of the earlier readings, skipping to the fourth Sunday reading as needed, in order to begin the antiphon readings on December 17.)

In addition to the daily reflections for the four weeks of Advent, this book includes special meditations to cover special feasts and commemorations during the seasons of Advent and Christmas. Substitute these readings for the daily reading as appropriate. These feasts include:

- Feast of St. Nicholas (December 6)
- Feast of the Immaculate Conception (December 8)
- Feast of Our Lady of Guadalupe (December 12)

Because this book is intended to be used from year to year, you may need to skip a few of the reflections in some years (or read two at a time, if you prefer). However you use this book, my prayer for you is that these reflections will provide a special time to ponder the wisdom of St. Teresa as it relates to each day's Scripture reading. Let the joyful anticipation of this season creep into your heart as you imitate the simplicity, humility, and love of this "saint of the slums," as you recall the miracle of the One who left behind unspeakable riches in order to walk among us for a time.

St. Teresa of Calcutta, pray for us!

Jesus, we trust in you!

First Week of Advent

Come, Lord Jesus!

We grow together in peace and kindness

First Sunday of Advent
FINDING PEACE WITHIN

Year A: Isaiah 2:1–5; Psalm 122:1–9; Romans 13:11–14; Matthew 24:37–44

Year B: Isaiah 63:16–19; 64:2–7; Psalm 80:2–19;

1 Corinthians 1:3–9; Mark 13:33–37

Year C: Jeremiah 33:14–16; Psalm 25:4–14;

1 Thessalonians 3:12—4:2; Luke 21:25–36

Peace be within your walls,
  and security within your towers.
For the sake of my relatives and friends
  I will say, "Peace be within you."
For the sake of the house of the LORD our God,
  I will seek your good.

—Psalm 122:7–9

During this first week of Advent, we look not to the past, to the Incarnation. Instead we look ahead, to the second coming of Christ. This "peace within" comes not from our own striving and grasping for power, but in loving surrender to the will of God, as revealed through Jesus Christ.

As Christians, every part of our life is oriented toward our place as citizens in the kingdom of God. We are called to love. We are called to serve. We are called to recognize the face of Christ in everyone around us, even our enemies, for the greater good of all.

In her lifetime, Mother Teresa frequently ministered to people in countries torn apart by war and civil unrest. Although she never met Mohandas

Gandhi, who was assassinated soon after she began her work, she borrowed from him the term "Co-Workers" to describe the laymen and women who assisted the Missionaries of Charity.[5] Like her Sisters, the Co-Workers tended to the immediate physical and spiritual needs of the impoverished and destitute, who were largely ignored by those in authority, to whom Mother Teresa appealed for consideration on their behalf.

Listen to the simple wisdom of this most beloved saint who wrote in a letter dated January 2, 1991, to then-Presidents George Bush and Saddam Hussein:

> It is not for us to destroy what God has given to us. Please, please let your mind and your will become the mind and will of God. You have the power to bring war into the world or to build peace. PLEASE CHOOSE THE WAY OF PEACE.[6]

We are not leaders of nations, and yet we hold in our power the ability to make peace in our corner of the world. Where have you experienced conflict this week at work, in your parish, as a volunteer, or among your family? Is there a "way of peace" that you are being called to walk? This path may not always be the most pleasant, or the most personally gratifying. It may involve letting go of some personal slight or forgiving an injustice—even if the other person is unwilling to meet you halfway.

As we begin our Advent journey, consider how God is calling you to choose the way of peace for the good of all…beginning with yourself.

A Moment to Reflect
- Where did you experience the "way of peace" in a special way?
- How will you show greater love and kindness today?

A Moment to Pray

Lord Jesus,
today you come to us not as a tiny stranger,
but as the Prince of Peace.
Take your place in our hearts, and stay there forever.
Help us to grow each day
in greater faith, hope, and love.
St. Teresa of Calcutta, pray for us!

Monday of the First Week of Advent
THE GIFT OF TRUST
Isaiah 2:1–5; Psalm 122:1–9; Matthew 8:5–11

> The centurion answered, "Lord, I am not worthy to have you come under my roof; but only speak the word, and my servant will be healed...." When Jesus heard him, he was amazed and said to those who followed him, "Truly I tell you, in no one in Israel have I found such faith."
>
> —Matthew 8:8, 10

Every time I say these words at Mass, I am reminded of the man who, despite the power and authority he wielded in the world, had the humility to recognize his own limitations. In the end, the desperate father threw himself on the mercy of his last—and, as it turns out, his greatest—hope.

We see this same simple humility and surrender in the life of St. Teresa—for her, it was her greatest source of peace and joy from the earliest days of her vocation. When she left the Loreto Convent to begin her mission to the poorest of the poor, she had only three plain saris and five rupees (at that time worth about one American dollar). But she had faith that God would guide and provide for her.[7]

This posture of trustful surrender is one that faces many of us at some point in our lives. Financial pressures, a child's illness, marital disharmony, or any number of other personal challenges bring us to the end of ourselves and cause us to prostrate ourselves—literally or emotionally—before the throne of grace. "Help me, God. I'm not worthy...but I'm asking you to help me anyway. Just because I know you can."

Imagine what faith it must have taken for Mother Teresa to take up her work in a new place, with so little in her purse. Instead she trusted in the benevolent hand of God.

This trust is a kind of gift that we can offer back to God. Like a child who places her little hand trustingly in the much larger one of her father's, our verbal expressions of assent and trust imitate, even in a pale way, the "Yes" of the centurion…and of the Mother of the Lord herself.

A Moment to Reflect
- In what area of your life has God been asking you to trust him? Have you found that easy or difficult to do?
- In what area of your life will you make a conscious effort to trust in Providence today?

A Moment to Pray
Jesus, I trust in you!
You are my peace, my hope, my joy.
Help me, Lord, when I am struggling to trust you.
Heal the hard and fearful places in my heart,
and give me joy.
St. Teresa of Calcutta, pray for us!

Tuesday of the First Week of Advent
BLESSED LITTLE THINGS
Isaiah 11:1–10; Psalm 72:1–17; Luke 10:21–24

At that same hour Jesus rejoiced in the Holy Spirit and said, "I thank you, Father, Lord of heaven and earth, because you have hidden these things from the wise and the intelligent and have revealed them to infants; yes, Father, for such was your gracious will.… No one knows who the Son is except the Father, or who the Father is except the Son and anyone to whom the Son chooses to reveal him."

—Luke 10:21–22

I attended my first Catholic Mass in my late twenties. To say it was something of a culture shock is to put it mildly. I didn't know the prayers or the hymns and had to pay careful attention to what others were doing to avoid drawing undue attention to myself. Until then I had always been the one behind the piano or teaching. Here I could only take it all in as I took my first tentative steps toward becoming a Catholic Christian.

Several years later, I experienced this same sense of starting over when I began graduate theology studies. While reciting Scripture came easily to me, the deeper, richer truths of the wider tradition of the Church were much harder to embrace at first. My teachers were patient, and God was faithful to reveal the truth to me. But first I had to be willing to start over, like a child.

Can you think of a time when you had to start over or help someone very dear to you face a new beginning? Perhaps the setback was financial, relational, or physical. The details don't matter as much as the detachment with which we face our present circumstances. There can be great blessing in letting go, cheerfully, knowing that God has a greater plan for us.

St. Teresa points to the story of Zacchaeus (see Luke 10:1–10) to remind us of the grace to be found in littleness and of the great treasures that the rich tax collector found by not letting his small stature deter him from seeing Jesus. She concludes,

> Likewise you and I…should be aware that we are small. We should make a decision to do little things with great love.[8]

The greatest "do overs" are taken not with giant steps, but with faltering, sometimes feeble steps of trust. Is God asking you to take such a step right now?

A Moment to Reflect

- When were your preconceived ideas and assumptions challenged? Where are you now being called to "embrace the mystery"?
- In what way can you imitate the example of Zacchaeus and become more childlike in your faith?"

A Moment to Pray

Lord Jesus,
as we get ready to celebrate Christmas,
the moment you appeared as a tiny, helpless infant,
help us to experience a renewed sense
of wonder and joy in this season,
and to rediscover innocence.
St. Teresa of Calcutta, pray for us!

Wednesday of the First Week of Advent
COMING HOME
Isaiah 25:6–10; Psalm 23:1–6; Matthew 15:29–37

On this mountain the LORD of hosts will make for all peoples
    a feast of rich food, a feast of well-matured wines,
    of rich food filled with marrow, of well-matured wines strained
       clear.
And he will destroy on this mountain
    the shroud that is cast over all peoples,
    the sheet that is spread over all nations;
    he will swallow up death forever.

—Isaiah 25:6–8

When the Missionaries of Charity celebrated the twenty-fifth anniversary of their order, Mother Teresa estimated that in that time she and her Sisters had picked up more than 36,000 people from the streets of Calcutta—of whom 17,000 had met "a very beautiful death."[9]

> Death can be something beautiful. It is like going home. He who dies in God goes home even though we naturally miss that person who has gone. But it is something beautiful. That person has gone home to God.[10]

The prophet Isaiah reminds us that God recognizes the sadness we feel at the death of loved ones. When grief prevents us from experiencing the joys of the season, we can think of those we love waiting for us, so we can experience that "feast of well-matured wines" together again in heaven, when at last we all are home.

For many of us, this thought will bring tears to our eyes as we think of the loved ones who have died, especially those who have died recently. Others will think of those whose minds are caught in the tangle of dementia or Alzheimer's disease. We grieve that they are no longer the people we remember, the people they once were. And yet, they are still beloved of God. Each of these losses speak to us of a much greater joy ahead.

What are some of the losses you have experienced this year? Where is the "gift" in this—and how can you honor the memory of that gift today? Look around you. Is there a mother in need of mothering, or a grandfather in need of grandchildren? How can you begin to redeem that loss by becoming home to one who needs it?

A Moment to Reflect

- One of the spiritual works of mercy is to "pray for the living and the dead." Has God brought someone to your mind this week who is in need of your prayers?
- Go to Mass this week and offer up a special prayer for those in purgatory who have no one to pray for them.

A Moment to Pray

Blessed Trinity,
draw me ever closer into that union of love,
where the blessed of all the ages worship you with perfect joy.
Help me to experience a foretaste of that joy today,
that I might share it with others.
St. Teresa of Calcutta, pray for us!

Thursday of the First Week of Advent
LOVE THAT IS FEARLESS
Isaiah 26:1–6; Psalm 118:8–27; Matthew 7:21–27

> It is better to take refuge in the LORD
>   than to put confidence in mortals.
> It is better to take refuge in the LORD
>   than to put confidence in princes.
>
> —Psalm 118:8–9

Although Mother Teresa was best known for her work in the slums of Calcutta, among the poorest of the poor who had no one else to help them, her Sisters also ministered in the "civilized" countries of the Western world that had social services in place. In these countries the Sisters often encountered a different type of poverty, a poverty of souls marked by loneliness and shame.

In her biography of Mother Teresa, Kathryn Spink recounts a story about the Sisters reaching out to an elderly woman who lived in "council housing" in the East End of London. When the sewers backed up, filling the flats with excrement, the Sisters persuaded the woman to let them in to help with the cleanup.

> Inside the woman's home, they found the two rooms covered in excrement, and [the Sisters] set to work—shoveling and cleaning up the mess, filling five large trash bags. "Do you still love me?" the woman asked the Sisters. "I love you even more now," was the unflinching response."[11]

Mother Teresa often insisted that her Sisters are not social workers. Love rushes in where "hired hands" would fear to tread.

What comes to mind for you when you hear this story? We do not need to go to foreign lands, or across the country—sometimes we do not even need to cross the street—to make these kinds of hidden sacrifices of love.

Think of those closest to you. What is the most distasteful, most frequently deferred chore that you could do that would say, "I love you even more" to the one you love best? Do that chore quietly and consistently, without drawing attention to it. Let your actions alone say, "I love you *this* much!"

A Moment to Reflect

- What are some of the unsavory or tiresome tasks love does willingly? What have you done to lift the burden of someone who needed a friend?
- How can you support ministry to the poor and homeless in your community? One idea is to fill small plastic bags with toiletries or snacks and perhaps a small-denomination gift card to a local grocery store. Keep them handy to give to souls in need.

A Moment to Pray

"Do small things with great love" was the motto of the great saints.

Lord, help me to be faithful in the small things,

so that one day you will say, "Well done!"

Give me courage, Lord, to act in love even when it's hard.

St. Teresa of Calcutta, pray for us!

Friday of the First Week of Advent
BEHOLD THE BEAUTY
Isaiah 29:17–24; Psalm 27:1–14; Matthew 9:27–31

One thing I asked of the LORD,
    that will I seek after:
to live in the house of the LORD
    all the days of my life,
to behold the beauty of the LORD,
    and to inquire in his temple.

—Psalm 27:4

The Eucharist is one of the great mysteries of the faith. Those who earnestly seek to know the will of God often find what they seek simply by sitting with Jesus in his Eucharistic presence in the adoration chapel.

Malcolm Muggeridge, the man whose BBC documentary and subsequent book would introduce the work of this diminutive saint to the world, received a letter from Mother Teresa in which she compares his search to that of the Pharisee and secret follower of Jesus, Nicodemus (see John 3:1–9). Kathryn Spink references this letter in her biography of St. Teresa:

> I am sure you will understand beautifully everything—if only you would become a little child in God's hands…. The personal love Christ has for you is infinite—the small difficulty you have regarding the Church is finite. Overcome the finite with the infinite. Christ has created you because he wanted you.[12]

Have you ever stopped to ponder the thought that the infinite God loves *you?* That he who created you believes you to be beautiful just as you are? That if you were the only person in the world, he still would have died just so he could spend eternity with you?

Such astounding beauty—this kind of lavish grace—to think that the creator of heaven and earth could not bear to be separated from us, even if it meant setting aside his glory for a time, just so we could see him and understand we have nothing to fear.

Jesus promised he would never leave or forsake us (Hebrews 13:5). But the first half of the verse unlocks the secret to seeing him truly: "Keep your lives free from the love of money, and be content with what you have; for he has said, 'I will never leave you or forsake you.'" When you search for beauty, do you know where to look?

A Moment to Reflect

- How have you taken time to listen for the voice of God in your heart? Does your life show you believe the Lord of the universe wants to speak with you?
- What will you do this week to prepare yourself to receive all the graces God wants to give you in the Eucharist?

A Moment to Pray

Holy Spirit, incline my heart
so that I might hear in a new and fresh way
the words God wants to speak to me.
Help me to see the beauty of the Lord in his sanctuary,
the gateway to heaven itself:
St. Teresa of Calcutta, pray for us!

Saturday of the First Week of Advent
HIDDEN GLORY
Isaiah 30:19–26; Psalm 147:1–6; Matthew 9:35–10:1–8

Then Jesus went about all the cities and villages, teaching in their synagogues, and proclaiming the good news of the kingdom, and curing every disease and every sickness. When he saw the crowds, he had compassion for them, because they were harassed and helpless, like sheep without a shepherd. Then he said to his disciples, "The harvest is plentiful, but the laborers are few; therefore ask the Lord of the harvest to send out laborers into his harvest."

—Matthew 9:35–38

The year I spent in Senegal, West Africa offered the simplest—yet the best—of all Christmases for me. Since Christmas was not a national holiday in that predominantly Muslim country—no carols on the radio, no Santas on every street corner—I had to find my own Christmas spirit.

One Saturday I bought a bag of oranges, peeling and feeding one of them to the elderly man who always sat just outside the *Supermarche*. His hands were leprous stumps. But his eyes lit up joyfully as I peeled each segment and put it in his mouth. Then he laughed out loud as the little children who had been begging in the area swarmed me—each determined to get a *cadeau* (gift) for themselves.

Years later, I still think about "Smiling Charlie," and wonder what more I could have done. We could not communicate—he spoke no English, and I spoke no Wolof. All I could do was bring him a little sweetness and joy in the name of the Infant King. In *One Heart Full of Love,* Mother Teresa recounts one of her own experiences among the lepers of India, at a Christmas party the Sisters had for them.

> We have thousands of lepers. They are so great, so beautiful inside in spite of their physical disfigurement.... I told them that they are a gift from God. God has a special love for them. He accepts them. An elderly man, completely disfigured by leprosy, said to me, "Say it again. That has been good for me. I have always heard that no one loves us. It is wonderful to know that God loves us."[13]

While Hansen's disease (leprosy) is almost unknown in the United States, there is no shortage of people who live on the margins and have given up hope because of some physical or psychological impairment.

Perhaps that person is someone very close to you who is afraid to reveal to the rest of the world feelings of worthlessness and disgust. The liberating truth, however, is that each of us is created in the very image of God. Each is invited to experience the joy of taking his or her rightful place in God's family. Will you ask God for the gift to see that person the way he does?

A Moment to Reflect

- All around the world, nearby and far away, are people who, like Mother Teresa, have dedicated their lives to serving God and the Church. Offer a prayer of thanks for someone you encountered this week.
- Ask the Lord to give you an opportunity to take a turn in the "harvest field" by sharing your faith with someone who needs it!

A Moment to Pray

Heavenly Father, I don't have to look very far
—barely outside my front door—
to see people who desperately need a word of hope,
who need to know about you.
Give me courage to open my mouth
and share my faith with someone today.
St. Teresa of Calcutta, pray for us!

Second Week of Advent

PREPARE THE WAY OF THE LORD:
WE GROW TOGETHER IN HOPEFUL COMMUNITY

Second Sunday of Advent
WELCOME HOME?

Year A: Isaiah 11:1–10; Psalm 72:1–17; Romans 15:4–9; Matthew 2:1–2
Year B: Isaiah 40:1–11; Psalm 85:9–14; 2 Peter 3:8–14; Mark 1:1–8
Year C: Baruch 5:1–9; Psalm 126:1–6; Philippians 1:4–6; Luke 3:1–6

May the God of steadfastness and encouragement grant you to
live in harmony with one another, in accordance with Christ
Jesus, that together you may with one voice glorify the God and
Father of our Lord Jesus Christ. Welcome one another, therefore,
just as Christ has welcomed you, for the glory of God.

—Romans 15:5–7

The next time you go to Mass, take a look around you for just a moment
before you take your seat. Notice those who walk a bit slowly, their heads
down as though deep in thought. Smile at the young woman who seems
just a little frazzled as she ushers her small children into the pew. Hold
the door for the elderly woman who comes to Mass all alone. Each of
these people has a story. Each of them has a burden. Each of them is your
brother, your sister. By acknowledging our companions around the table
of the Lord, members of his body, we honor Christ as well. Our unity
must not be merely theological, but real, as together we turn to worship
God, the source of all love.

The Catholic faith is not simply a personal moral code or an individual
set of beliefs; our faith is by nature relational, based on unity and communion. "How can you claim to love God, whom you have never seen, if you

do not love your brother, whom you have seen?" Jesus asks us. Similarly, St. Teresa reminds us:

> This neglect to love brings spiritual poverty. Maybe in our own family we have somebody who is feeling lonely, who is feeling sick, who is feeling worried. Are we there? Are we willing to give until it hurts in order to be with our families, or do we put our own interests first?… We must remember that love begins at home and that "the future of humanity passes through the family."[14]

For many people, the word *family* is a painful one. It brings up powerful images of both belonging and rejection, of caring and despairing, of the need to share openly, and the fear of disclosing too much.

Although human relationships so often fall short of what we need, our disappointment does not stop the longing. That longing is the desire that God has placed in each of us to belong, more specifically…to belong to him. "You have made us for yourself, O God," said St. Augustine. "And our hearts are restless until they rest in you."

A Moment to Reflect
- Where did we experience a sense of being part of God's family in a special way?
- How will we show the reason for our hope and our commitment to our family—both those nearby and far away?

A Moment to Pray
Lord Jesus, you are the cause of our hope.
By leaving heaven and coming to earth

to live within the Holy Family,
you made us part of an eternal communion of love.
Help us to reflect that hope and love
to everyone we meet.
St. Teresa of Calcutta, pray for us!

Monday of the Second Week of Advent
CHOOSING ONENESS
Isaiah 35:1–10; Psalm 85:9–14; Luke 5:27–26

And the ransomed of the LORD shall return,
    and come to Zion with singing;
everlasting joy shall be upon their heads;
    they shall obtain joy and gladness,
    and sorrow and sighing shall flee away.

—Isaiah 35:10

"You can't go home again." Whether it's a college student returning to see his parents at Christmas, a family visiting their home parish after moving away, or someone attending a high school reunion, we become aware of the truth that a departure sets in motion a series of events that alters forever the nature of the relationship between the one who leaves and the one who was left.

The prophet Isaiah tells of the exiles returning to rebuild after years of captivity. Notice the phrase he uses: "they shall obtain joy and gladness." The joyful singing prevails as the sorrow and sighing "flee away." It is a process, requiring a silent acknowledgement of the necessity for ransom, of all that was lost in the interim. So if a catch in your throat arises as you sing, if your eyes glisten too brightly to see the words clearly, be not afraid. The joy is coming yet.

In the case of Mother Teresa, finding her spiritual family meant losing every single member of her family of origin, left behind in Albania as she sought God's will in the slums of Calcutta. It is perhaps because of that painful loss that she went to such great lengths to build community and empathy among her own Sisters as well as her Co-Workers, each of them living in solidarity with the others no matter where on earth they lived. Said St. Teresa:

> Our first great responsibility is to be a family, a community, revealing first to one another something of God's love and concern and tenderness.[14]

To what family have you been called? Have you been giving yourself as wholeheartedly as you would like? What have you taught your own children about what it means to be part of a family?

A Moment to Reflect
- When have you felt nostalgic about things you experienced in holidays past? Where is "home" for you?
- What can you do this week to recapture some of those favorites? What can you share, remember, and celebrate?

A Moment to Pray
Lord, thank you for the gift of memory,
even the sad memories that are a part of my life's story.
Thank you, too, for the opportunities I have every day
to share my joy as a redeemed member of the body of Christ!
St. Teresa of Calcutta, pray for us!

Tuesday of the Second Week of Advent
EVERY VALLEY LIFTED UP
Isaiah 40:1–11; Psalm 96–1–13; Matthew 18:12–14

Every valley shall be lifted up,
   and every mountain and hill be made low;
the uneven ground shall become level,
   and the rough places a plain.
Then the glory of the LORD shall be revealed,
   and all people shall see it together,
   for the mouth of the LORD has spoken.

—Isaiah 40:4–5

Every year about this time my husband and I take the kids to a neighborhood church that hosts an annual community singing of Handel's *Messiah*. A respectable orchestra crams into the choir loft, and as the house lights dim just a bit, the tenor soloist proclaims these ancient words of the prophet, thrilling us as we ponder celebrating once again the Incarnation, the fulfillment of this prophecy.

This remembering as a community is an indispensable part of the joy of Advent. We are not individual lights flickering in the darkness, all too readily snuffed out by a wayward gust. No, like note building on note to a great crescendo, we stand together as the music washes over us, until at last we sing with delirious joy the final "Hallelujah!"

This annual Advent tradition reminds me over and over again how important it is to observe such rituals that extend beyond the confines of our own homes. To be Catholic is to give ourselves wholeheartedly to the mystery that we are a part of something infinitely greater than ourselves, to accomplish as part of a body more than we could do on our own.

> What we are doing is just a drop in the ocean. But if that drop was not in the ocean I think the ocean would be less because of that missing drop.[15]

Especially during the Christmas holidays, it's easy to become overwhelmed with all the activities and expenses associated with keeping in touch with those who are only on the periphery of our lives the rest of the year. Think of how you might be "just a drop"—how you might connect just as meaningfully in *small* and *simple* ways, to spend time hidden in the valley with that Infant King who wants nothing more than to spend some time with you and reveal to you his glory.

A Moment to Reflect
- What are some of the activities and projects of this season that captured your attention that, in retrospect, could have been simplified or eliminated entirely?
- How will you be "just a drop in the ocean" of God's mercy this week?

A Moment to Pray
Blessed Trinity, you are community at heart—
an eternal offering of self-gift.
Help me to imitate that kind of love,
and to give of myself whenever I have the opportunity,
for as long as I am able to give.
St. Teresa of Calcutta, pray for us!

Wednesday of the Second Week of Advent
THE ELEVATED HEART
Isaiah 40:25–31; Psalm 103:1–10; Matthew 11:28–30

Those who wait for the LORD shall renew their strength,
> they shall mount up with wings like eagles,
they shall run and not be weary,
> they shall walk and not faint.

—Isaiah 40:31

More than a decade has passed since my husband and I became "instant parents" to a sibling group from inner-city Detroit. When I look at the pictures from those first few months, baking cookies and decorating our gingerbread house, I remember the bone-weariness that, more than once, made me question what had possessed me to think I had what it took to help these kids who had lost their first family at such a tender age.

In some respects, we're not that different from other families—many parents can relate to that bone-tiredness. No doubt the Blessed Mother, holy as she was, dreaded at times the thought of riding that donkey mile after endless mile to reach the fulfillment of God's promise. If we dwell too much on the circumstances, we lose out on the joy; when we elevate our minds and hearts, we find that God has given us the strength to persevere.

In their book *Suffering into Joy,* Eileen and Kathleen Egan, OSB, speak of the extraordinary sacrifices of Mother Teresa's family, who remained trapped in Albania after their "Agnes" left to respond to God's call. Only her brother Lazar, who had married an Italian woman, was later reunited with her when in 1960 Mother Teresa went to Rome to request official recognition of the Missionaries of Charity.[16] Though she was confident her family would be restored to her in heaven, she felt the loss acutely—and still, she continued to walk in the way God had shown her to go.

> We belong to Jesus and obedience is our strength. You must do small acts of obedience with great love. Obedience is not a joke. It is a sacrifice. The more you love God, the more you will obey. Obedience is a cross—pick up your cross and follow him. Everyone in the world has to obey in one way or another. People are forced to obey or they will lose their jobs. But we obey out of love for Jesus.[17]

A Moment to Reflect

- What are some of your favorite memories of Advents past?
- What was the moment this week you most despaired of getting through the day? How were you able to redirect your outlook?
- What can you do out of love for Jesus this week?

A Moment to Pray

Lord, the price of obedience can be very dear at times—
but still I want to follow.
Thank you for the tender mercies
of those who graced my life for a time.
Help me to be a source of grace
for someone else.
St. Teresa of Calcutta, pray for us!

Thursday of the Second Week of Advent
THIRSTY
Isaiah 41:13–20; Psalm 145:1–13; Matthew 11:11–15

When the poor and needy seek water,
and there is none,
and their tongue is parched with thirst,
I the LORD will answer them,
I the God of Israel will not forsake them.

—Isaiah 41:17

"I thirst" were among the last words that the Lord spoke from the cross (John 19:28). In a wonderful way, these lines from today's first reading tie together the two great mysteries of the Christian faith: the Incarnation, the Word made flesh, and the Paschal Mystery, the Lord's passion that redeems and restores us. No Advent is complete until we consider not just *the reality* of God made flesh, but *the reason* for this miracle. Just as there is no Easter without Good Friday, so there is no Good Friday without Christmas. This is what fills us with such hope during Advent.

"I thirst" was also the theme of a special card that St. Teresa passed out to those she encountered to remind them of the passionate and infinite love of Jesus. The words he spoke from the cross, "I thirst" (John 19:28), spoke not only of the physical torment he endured, but of the yearning that kept him there, suffering on our behalf.

Jesus is God, therefore His love, His Thirst, is infinite. He, the creator of the universe, asked for the love of His creatures. He thirsts for our love.... These words: "I Thirst"—do they echo in our souls?[18]

The image of the Lord "thirsting" for souls, even as he pours himself out, body and blood, to infuse us with eternal life is a powerful one. Just as Mary quenched the thirst of her infant Son with milk from her own body, so we must make an offering of our very selves in gratitude and love.

A Moment to Reflect

- Imagine standing beneath a crucifix at your parish and hearing the Lord say to you: "I thirst." How would you respond?
- Go to the Missionaries of Charity Fathers website and read the "I Thirst" prayer aloud. Which line is most meaningful to you?

A Moment to Pray

Lord Jesus, thank you for filling the thirst in my heart
for love, for understanding, for family.
Help me to recognize the spiritual thirst all around me,
and help me to do my part to meet that need.
St. Teresa of Calcutta, pray for us!

Friday of the Second Week of Advent

SPREADING THE LOVE

Isaiah 48:17–19; Psalm 1:1–6; Matthew 11:16–19

> For John came neither eating nor drinking, and they say, "He has a demon"; the Son of Man came eating and drinking, and they say, "Look, a glutton and a drunkard, a friend of tax collectors and sinners!" Yet wisdom is vindicated by her deeds.
>
> —Matthew 11:18–19

There is nothing quite like the Christmas holidays to bring to a boil family tensions that simmer just beneath the surface the rest of the year. The personal differences between family members—marital status, social habits, religious preferences, and financial concerns—can make it difficult to connect meaningfully on a personal level, especially when misunderstandings and prejudices emerge.

Yes, spending precious vacation time sitting elbow-to-elbow with extended family who find your very presence an affront to their most cherished beliefs ("What do you *mean* you didn't put marshmallows in the sweet 'taters?") is not exactly a welcome prospect. And yet, as St. Teresa reminds us, this is exactly what we have been called to do.

> O God, the Father of us all, you ask every one of us to spread
> Love where the poor are humiliated, joy where the Church is
> brought low,
> And reconciliation where people are divided.[19]

"Wisdom is vindicated by her deeds," the Gospel tells us. The things we do to express love even for those who are hardest to love, are not wasted on God. Willing hands at cleanup time, generous sharing of resources, and thoughtful cards and remembrances have a way of softening hearts as well. The harder it is to give, the greater the joy of the angels, for "Truly I tell you, just as you did it to one of the least of these who are members of my family, you did it to me" (Matthew 25:40).

A Moment to Reflect

- Who was the hardest person for you to love? What did you do? Given the opportunity, is there anything you would do differently next time?
- Is there someone in your life with whom you are in conflict? Is there something you can do to love "the least of these" in Jesus's name?

A Moment to Pray

Lord, you see it all.
You know what I am up against.
Give me the grace to spread your sweetness
wherever I go in the weeks ahead.
Jesus, I trust in you!
St. Teresa of Calcutta, pray for us!

Second Saturday of Advent
GRACE CHASERS
Sirach 48:1–11; Psalm 80:1–19; Matthew 17:9–13

Then Elijah arose, a prophet like fire,
and his word burned like a torch.

...

By the word of the Lord he shut up the heavens,
and also three times brought down fire.
How glorious you were, Elijah, in your wondrous deeds!
Whose glory is equal to yours?

—Sirach 48:1, 2–4

In today's Gospel reading (Matthew 17:9–13), the Lord revealed that John the Baptist had been the "Elijah" the scribes had foretold would precede the Messiah. But "they did not recognize him" (17:12), just as the religious establishment of his day did not recognize Jesus as the Son of God, the long-awaited Messiah.

Part of the reason such greatness flies under the radar of most people is because of the form it takes. In the kingdom of Heaven, the first shall be last, the greatest least, and the master is the servant of all. During this season of Advent we anticipate the greatest example of this mysterious paradox: how the king of heaven and earth was willing to make himself so small and helpless. Had trumpets blazed from heaven and fiery chariots fallen to earth, perhaps his message would have fallen on ears more predisposed to hear it. Instead, he flew "under the radar" as an ordinary man with an extraordinary mission...much like his cousin, the kindred spirit of Elijah whom St. Teresa called the "other wire."

Our Lady was the most wonderful wire! She surrendered completely to God, became full of grace, and the current—the grace of God—flowed through her. The moment she was filled with this current, she went to Elizabeth's house to connect that other wire—John—to the current—Jesus. And Elizabeth said, "This child leapt with joy in my womb at your voice." Let us ask Mary to help make that current within us so that Jesus can use us around the world to connect the hearts of men with the current, Jesus.[20]

On their own, two sets of wire (one charged with current, the other dead) can look exactly alike. What makes them useful is being plugged into the power source. In the same way, we can go through the same motions week after week out of a sense of tradition or duty. It isn't until we acknowledge our own powerlessness and ask God to fill us with grace that, like Elijah and John, we become conduits of that grace to others.

A Moment to Reflect
- Sometimes God speaks to us in subtle ways—a line of Scripture or a timely word from a friend. How has God made his presence known to you this week?
- How will you "connect" with those around you, to share with them the joy of the Advent season?

A Moment to Pray
O Eternal Mystery,
reveal yourself to my heart today.
Help me to see the signs of your love and compassion,
and to share those with others as well.
St. Teresa of Calcutta, pray for us!

Third Week of Advent
ARISE, MOST RADIANT DAWN!
WE GROW TOGETHER IN JOY AND COURAGE

Third Sunday of Advent
ROSE SUNDAY
Year A: Isaiah 35:1–10; Psalm 146:6–10; James 5:7–10; Matthew 11:2–11
Year B: Isaiah 6:1–11; Luke 1:46–54; 1 Thessalonians 5:24; John 1:6–28
Year C: Zephaniah 3:14–18; Psalm 12:2–6; Philippians 4:4–7; Luke 3:10–18

For waters shall break forth in the wilderness,
   and the streams in the desert;…
And the ransomed of the LORD shall return,
   and come to Zion with singing;
everlasting joy shall be upon their heads;
   they shall obtain joy and gladness,
   and sorrow and sighing shall flee away.

—Isaiah 35:6, 10

The third Sunday of Advent is known as "Rose Sunday," a bit of brightness and joy in the middle of this season. By this time, as we light two purple and a single rose candle on the Advent wreath, the artificial clamor and forced frivolity of the season can begin to grate as we stuff more and more activity into already overcrowded schedules. There is always more to do and not nearly enough time to *be*.

This week, take courage and reclaim the present moment for the gift that it is. Take some time away from the daily rush. Have a few friends for a mini-retreat of afternoon tea and cake, or take the family outside to make snow angels, or into the kitchen for a little tea or cocoa. Find a way to reconnect with the simple joy of living as we recall the gentle words of St. Teresa, who urges us to experience the unadorned presence of the living God.

> If your heart is full of worldly things, you cannot hear the voice of God. But when you have listened to his voice in the silence of your heart, then your heart is filled. Then, from the fullness of the heart the mouth will speak.... When you look at people, they must be able to see God in your eyes.[21]

This kind of purposeful, intentional living is countercultural. It might also be counterintuitive if you are a multitasking specialist who measures the success of a day by the number of items checked off a to-do list. But this is a different kind of victory, the success of a well-ordered life.

A Moment to Reflect
- What caused your heart to experience joy this week?
- Rose Sunday is also called *Gaudete* (Rejoice) Sunday. Have you praised God and rejoiced over his many blessings?

A Moment to Pray
Lord Jesus, you are the cause of all joy.
We praise you for your many blessings,
and thank you for your faithfulness to our family.
Help us to be courageous and joyful
in the choices we make each day,
to serve and love you better.
St. Teresa of Calcutta, pray for us!

Monday of the Third Week of Advent
PUT THE PAST IN THE PAST

Numbers 24:2–7, 15–17; Psalm 25:4–9; Matthew 21:23–27

Be mindful of your mercy, O LORD, and of your steadfast love,
    for they have been from of old.
Do not remember the sins of my youth or my transgressions;
    according to your steadfast love remember me,
    for your goodness' sake, O LORD!

—Psalm 25:6–7

The prophet Balaam is the protagonist in one of my favorite Bible stories—Balaam and his inscrutable donkey (see Numbers 22:22–40, which precedes today's first reading). When God sent an angel to stand in the road to detain the determined Balaam, the donkey saw the celestial being and drew back, fearful. Not until God opened the prophet's eyes and caused the wise little donkey to speak did Balaam repent of his foolish mission.

As children of God, we often act on negative motivations like pride, fear, or simple desire—and just as often, live to regret it. What a blessing it is, then, when a courageous soul steps up to block our path, to speak words that challenge and even deter us from doing what we know in our hearts is wrong.

The evil one does all he can to dissuade us from listening to God's harbinger of joy. After all, he wants to hold those regrets over us, to keep us ashamed and running away from God. But God does not hold against us the mistakes of the past, and it is not beyond this "hound of heaven" to send us signs to get our attention and put us back on the right path. As Mother Teresa reminds us, we can defeat the stranglehold of evil with joyful hearts.

> Joy is one of the best safeguards against temptation. The devil is a carrier of dust and dirt and he uses every opportunity to throw what he has at us. But joy protects us from this dirt. Jesus is with us there in our joy.[22]

Perhaps there is someone in your life who has wandered away from the path, who needs a little encouragement to leave the past in the past and start over. Are you willing to be God's little donkey and speak words of courage and reconciliation?

A Moment to Reflect
- Is there anything you did that you now regret and need to tell God about—possibly in confession?
- How will you practice joy in the face of temptation?

A Moment to Pray
Heavenly Father,
sometimes life would be much easier
if you sent an angel to stand in my way
each time I was about to go down a wrong path!
Instead you wait patiently
for me to ask for help and forgiveness.
Thank you for your mercy and your love.
St. Teresa of Calcutta, pray for us!

Tuesday of the Third Week of Advent
CHOOSING JOY
Zephaniah 3:1–13; Psalm 34:2–23; Matthew 21:28–32

O fear the LORD, you his holy ones,
  for those who fear him have no want.
The young lions suffer want and hunger,
  but those who seek the LORD lack no good thing.
                                        —Psalm 34:9–10

"God is not a bubblegum machine—put in a prayer, get what you want!" This was my mother's advice when I expressed a childish determination to get God to deliver on something she couldn't give me. Though I didn't appreciate it at the time, she was trying to teach me something important about the connection between happiness and contentment.

In their book *Suffering Into Joy,* the Egan sisters recount a story about the Missionaries of Charity in which the Sisters, running a just-opened center in the United States, went to work tearing up newly installed rugs from the floors. Knowing that their Sisters in other parts of the world did not enjoy such luxuries, "the Sisters politely explained to the donors that a more fitting use could be found for the carpeting."[23]

This detachment from luxury and identification with the poor they were trying to reach allowed the Missionaries of Charity to minister with joy even in the most poverty-stricken places in the world. For them, joy is a simple choice, as St. Teresa says:

> In Bethlehem, the angel announced tidings of great joy.… Joy
> was the password of the first Christians. In various ways, St. Paul
> repeats the refrain of joy: "Rejoice in the Lord always, again I say,
> rejoice." Remember, joy is not simply a matter of temperament,
> but of choice; it must be cultivated.[24]

Is there something intrinsically evil about wall-to-wall carpeting? Of course not. God is a generous God and expects us to be good stewards of what we possess in order to live out the demands of our own vocation. By holding lightly to our possessions, and being generous with those in need, we are free to love as we ought and will escape the trap of pride, envy, and greed. Above all, we will be free to choose joy.

A Moment to Reflect
- When have you asked God for something that, in retrospect, might have been selfish or robbed you of contentment?
- How will you practice the virtue of contentment this week?

A Moment to Pray
Blessed, Holy Trinity,
your angels travel throughout the world,
guarding and guiding your children
in good times and bad.
Help me to see my circumstances this week
as a cause for joy,
an opportunity to practice contentment in everything I do.
St. Teresa of Calcutta, pray for us!

Wednesday of the Third Week of Advent

IN THE GARDEN OF MEMORIES

Isaiah 45:6–25; Psalm 85:9–14; Luke 7:18–23

> And he [Jesus] answered them, "Go and tell John what you have
> seen and heard: the blind receive their sight, the lame walk, the
> lepers are cleansed, the deaf hear, the dead are raised, the poor
> have good news brought to them. And blessed is anyone who
> takes no offense at me."
>
> —Luke 7:22–23

A small upright piano stands in the corner of the common area in my
mother's memory care facility. Most days when I go in to visit, the resi-
dents are gathered around the big-screen television about fifty feet away,
their backs to the piano. Most have their eyes closed, their minds lost in
some long-ago time.

"Go ahead," the activities director encourages me, and Mom and I take
the old hymnal from the bench and sit down. Because of the distance,
I'm unable to visit more than once a month, but each time the response
is the same: first heads turn; then chairs inch their way closer, seemingly
reluctant to do anything that might stop the music. One scratchy voice
joins in a tune. Then another. Mom beams at me, alert and delighted to
escape, even for a few moments, to a happier time. "And he walks with me
and he talks with me, and tells me I am his own. And the joy we share as
we tarry there, none other has ever known."[25] My mother's smile reminds
me of St. Teresa's words:

> To smile at someone who is sad; to visit, even for a little while, someone who is lonely; to give someone shelter from the rain with our umbrella; to read something for someone who is blind: these and others can be the very small things that give…our love of God concrete expression to the poor.[26]

To be perfectly honest, it doesn't seem like enough, driving or flying twelve hundred miles every month or so, just to spend a couple of hours with the woman who dedicated so much of her life to me. But each time I show up, her face lights up and time stops, if only for a little while. And in that moment, as we talk about the good old times, which now blend so seamlessly with the present, we have a taste of pure joy there in our garden of memories.

A Moment to Reflect
- When did you "bring Jesus" to someone who needs him or help alleviate someone's pain?
- What small thing could you do to make this season a little brighter for someone who is lonely or suffering?

A Moment to Pray
Jesus, you announced the kingdom of God
through mighty miracles
as well as your own quiet, gentle presence.
Help me to recognize suffering wherever I see it,
and to imitate your love for the poor.
St. Teresa of Calcutta, pray for us!

Thursday of the Third Week of Advent
GOING FOR THE GOLD
Isaiah 54:1–10; Psalm 30:2–13; Luke 7:24–30

When John's messengers had gone, Jesus began to speak to the
crowds about John [the Baptist]: "What did you go out into the
wilderness to look at? A reed shaken by the wind? What then did
you go out to see? Someone dressed in soft robes? Look, those
who put on fine clothing and live in luxury are in royal palaces.
What then did you go out to see? A prophet? Yes, I tell you, and
more than a prophet. This is the one about whom it is written,
"'See, I am sending my messenger ahead of you,
    who will prepare your way before you.'"

—Luke 7:24–27

In his encyclical *Laudato Si*, Pope Francis writes: "When people become
self-centered and self-enclosed, their greed increases. The emptier a person's
heart is, the more he or she needs things to buy, own and consume."[27]

St. Teresa's life amply demonstrates that the opposite is also true: the
fuller the heart, the greater the possibility of being truly content, even
with very little. Looking into the eyes of Mother Teresa and her Sisters,
the first thing you notice isn't rough-hewn saris and simple sandals. The
first thing you see…is the joy.

As St. Teresa reminds us:

Let us not look for substitutes which restore to us the wealth
we have given up. Christ, who emptied himself to work out

our redemption, calls us: To listen to the voice of the poor…
to make reparation for the selfishness and greed of man, craving
for earthly riches, and power to the point of injustice to others.[28]

But what's the point? Isn't it better to improve the lot of the poor, than to
imitate them in their poverty? Perhaps, except for those whom the Lord
urges to "follow me" even in his poverty. They have been promised something infinitely more valuable than what they have relinquished: "And
everyone who has left houses or brothers or sisters or father or mother or
children or fields, for my name's sake, will receive a hundredfold, and will
inherit eternal life" (Matthew 19:29).

A Moment to Reflect

- Pope Francis is frequently in the news for the way he talks about and
  reaches out to the poor, just as St. Francis did before him. Think
  about what you heard in the news about the pope this week. Did his
  actions prompt you to turn away…or to look more closely at your
  faith and how you practice it?
- If you have not already done so, consider reading and reflecting upon
  Laudato Si, and consider how you might better apply its teachings to
  your life.

A Moment to Pray

Holy Spirit,
come and fill my heart with love and compassion,
that I might be focused
not on being extravagant with those closest to me
but on true charity toward those who need it most.
St. Teresa of Calcutta, pray for us!

Friday of the Third Week of Advent
MY HIDING PLACE
Isaiah 56:1–8; Psalm 67:2–8; John 5:33–36

[John the Baptist] was a burning and shining lamp, and you were willing to rejoice for a while in his light. But I have a testimony greater than John's. The works that the Father has given me to complete, the very works that I am doing, testify on my behalf that the Father has sent me.

—John 5:35–36

When my children were little, I used to tell them that God sends every baby into the world with three things: a gift to share, a burden to carry, and a job to do. When that job is done, the job he entrusted us—and only us—to do, he takes us back to heaven to spend eternity with him there. The gifts, burdens, and jobs he gives to each of us are as unique as we are. Not better. Not worse. Just different. The one thing we all share in common: He is the source of our strength.

We see this in the life of John the Baptist, the "burning and shining lamp" that heralded the way of Christ. And we see it in St. Teresa of Calcutta and her Sisters. You and I could never have accomplished all she did in her lifetime because that was hers, and not ours, to do. Her life was not more important to God than ours are, and though her burdens were great—so was the strength God gave her to carry them.

In the following excerpt from *One Heart Full of Love,* we learn the source of that great strength of Mother Teresa and her Sisters, and what it was that kept them going even in the most desperate circumstances: They knew, beyond a shadow of a doubt, that Jesus had sent them, and Jesus was among them.

> In the beginnings of our congregation, we used to have adoration of the Blessed Sacrament once a week. At our last general meeting or convocation, there was a unanimous consensus on the part of all the sisters that there should be daily adoration. We now have an hour of adoration before the Blessed Sacrament every day. Upon returning home, we spend an hour alone worshiping Jesus in the Blessed Sacrament. I believe that this has been the greatest gift to our congregation. It is something that has worked important changes in our lives.[29]

As we move into the "O Antiphons" and the final week of Advent, take a moment to ponder whether Jesus is your strength, too. In the times when we feel depleted, what our souls need most is a quiet hour, just soaking in his strength. Thus fortified, we can lift any burden, do any task. We can do great, little things for God.

A Moment to Reflect
- Was there a time you felt your energy flagging, your spirit sinking in discouragement, and you found yourself unable to share a part of yourself you had given a dozen times before? What does today's reading suggest to you?
- Where do you think you will need his strength the most? How will you eke out some time to fortify yourself for the task?

A Moment to Pray

You are my hiding place, O God.
You fill my heart with songs of deliverance.
Even when I am afraid I will trust in you.
St. Teresa of Calcutta, pray for us!

Fourth Week of Advent
CELEBRATE THE HOLY FAMILY!
WE GROW TOGETHER IN LOVE,
AND MAKE OUR HEARTS READY FOR JESUS

Note: There is no Saturday of the Fourth Week of Advent. See the dated entries for December 17–23. The reflection for the Fourth Sunday of Advent should be used on the Sunday that falls within that span.

Fourth Sunday of Advent
PEACEFUL FORGIVENESS

Year A: Isaiah 7:10–14; Psalm 24:1–10; Romans 1:1–7; Matthew 1:18–24
Year B: 2 Samuel 7:1–16; Psalm 89:2–29; Romans 16:25–27; Luke 1:26–38
Year C: Micah 5:1–4; Psalm 80:2–19; Hebrews 10:5–10; Luke 1:39–45

> Now the birth of Jesus the Messiah took place in this way. When his mother Mary had been engaged to Joseph, but before they lived together, she was found to be with child from the Holy Spirit. Her husband Joseph, being a righteous man and unwilling to expose her to public disgrace, planned to dismiss her quietly. But just when he had resolved to do this, an angel of the Lord appeared to him in a dream and said, "Joseph, son of David, do not be afraid to take Mary as your wife, for the child conceived in her is of the Holy Spirit. She will bear a son, and you are to name him Jesus, for he will save his people from their sins."
>
> —Matthew 1:18–21

This story from Matthew's Gospel recalls a particular moment in the story of the Nativity in which we see the shadow of the glory, the human struggle behind the miracle of the Incarnation. St. Joseph's struggle to reconcile Mary's story with his own sense of decency speaks to me not of tinsel-kissed tableaus, but of a very different kind of Christmas reality: those somber souls who can scarcely hide their broken heart, wrenching loss, or the fact that they are at some other life-altering crossroads, such as the one St. Joseph faced.

Even Mother Teresa, who so often counseled others to always smile at Jesus, knew how it felt to feel far away from God:

> I remember when I was leaving home fifty years ago—my mother was dead set against me leaving home and becoming a sister. In the end, when she realized that this was what God wanted from her and from me, she said something very strange: 'Put your hand in his hand and walk all alone with him.' This is exactly our way of life. We may be surrounded by people, yet our vocation is really lived out alone with Jesus.[30]

On this the fourth Sunday of Advent, we are reminded that to grow in love does not necessarily mean to *feel* more loving, but to *choose* it regardless of the feeling. The way can be very hard and lonely at times. But we can ask God for the courage to persevere.

A Moment to Reflect

- When did you feel strongly God wanted you to do something, yet you struggled to say yes? How does today's Gospel speak to your situation?
- In these final days of preparation, what do you still need to do to get ready to receive the gift of the Infant King?

A Moment to Pray

Blessed Mother,
who labored to bring forth the Light of the World
from the darkness,
pray for us,
that the love of Christ would shine in our hearts,

and in the cradle of our home.
St. Teresa of Calcutta, pray for us!

December 17
O WISDOM[31]
Genesis 49:2–10; Psalm 72:1–4, 7–8, 17; Matthew 1:1–17

O Wisdom of our God Most High,
guiding creation with power and love:
come to teach us the path of knowledge!

In the book of Wisdom, we read that she (wisdom) "reaches mightily from one end of the earth to the other, and she orders all things well" (8:1). As one of the gifts of the Holy Spirit (see Isaiah 11:2), wisdom infuses learning and transcends mere experience to provide the steady light we need to walk confidently in the way God has shown us.

In *Mother Teresa: Her People and Her Work,* Desmond Doig recounts the story of a dying woman who brought her little grandson to Shishu Bhavan, an orphanage founded and run by the Missionaries of Charity. His own parents had already died, and with no other family, his grandmother asked if the little boy could live in the children's home. Sister Agnes recalls:

> When he was small, whenever Mother used to ask him what he was going to do when he grew up, he used to say, "I will become Mother Teresa." So Mother put him in a seminary and he became a priest.[32]

This story reminds us that the way of wisdom is not always the easy way, or the path of least resistance. Often a knot of pain and sacrifice is a kernel that feeds the tree as it grows and produces its harvest. In this, too, "she orders all things well."

A Moment to Reflect

- What have you done to help a child find a path to wisdom? How have you used the gift of wisdom you received from the Holy Spirit through the sacraments of baptism and confirmation?
- How might you exercise this gift of the Spirit in your own life?

A Moment to Pray

Holy Spirit, Source of all Wisdom,
kindle in my heart the fire of your wisdom,
so that I might walk the path You have for me
with confidence, trust, and joy.
St. Teresa of Calcutta, pray for us!

December 18
O Mighty Lord
Jeremiah 23:5–8; Psalm 71:1–2, 12–13, 18–19; Matthew 1:18–24

O Leader of the House of Israel,
giver of the Law to Moses on Sinai:
come to rescue us with your mighty power!

This antiphon touches upon the story in Exodus in which Moses is drawn into the presence of God through a flaming bush in the desert—a bush that "was blazing, yet it was not consumed" (Exodus 3:2). Unwilling to leave his children in bondage, God commissions Moses to release his people from bondage under the powerful hand of Pharaoh (3:10–12).

At the beatification of his friend who became Blessed Teresa of Calcutta, Pope John II remembered her as one who raised up those in a different kind of bondage:

Mother Teresa…wanted to be a sign of "God's love, God's presence and God's compassion," and so remind all of the value and dignity of each of God's children, "created to love and be loved." Thus was Mother Teresa "bringing souls to God and God to souls" and satiating Christ's thirst, especially for those most in need, those whose vision of God had been dimmed by suffering and pain.[33]

During Advent we anticipate our own release, not through the Law of Moses but through the atoning death of God Incarnate. At the same time, we remember that by grace we also now walk on holy ground, in the presence of God and the company of the saints who surround and intercede for us.

These are the faithful warriors who stand with us as we resist the evil one who seeks to ensnare us, who whispers in our ears that it is no use, that we should just give up the fight. And in a way, that is exactly what we need to do: to toss our hands up and throw ourselves on the infinite mercy. The battle is the Lord's!

O Mighty Lord, O Leader of the House of Israel, we await your coming with joyful hope!

A Moment to Reflect

- By giving the Law, God provided a training ground for those who for too long had been under the unrelenting authority of a far harsher master. Is there some aspect of the teachings of the Church that you struggle to see as a sign of grace, protecting you from far greater bondage?

- Mother Teresa frequently spoke of obedience as a way of happiness and freedom. In what area of your life can you entrust your life more fully to God through a simple act of trust and obedience?

A Moment to Pray

St. Teresa, you frequently offered this prayer of faith:

"Humility of the heart of Jesus, fill my heart."[34]

Pray for me, that this would become my constant prayer as well.

St. Teresa of Calcutta, pray for us!

December 19
O ROOT OF JESSE
Judges 13:2–7, 24–25; Psalm 71:3–6, 16–17; Luke 1:5–25

O Root of Jesse's stem,
sign of God's love for all his people:
come to save us without delay!

When we sing the line of the popular Advent hymn,
"O come, O Rod of Jesse's stem,
From ev'ry foe deliver them."[35]

The significance of this phrase is lost on many of us. In reality, this line contains the reason for our joy, for it reminds us that no one—*no one*—is beyond the reach of God's mercy.

When the unfaithful kingdom of Israel fell to the Assyrians (around 750 BC), Isaiah prophesied about a King who would one day arise from Jesse's stem (Isaiah 11:1–2).[36] That prophesy offered a beacon of hope to them…and to us today, as we read in the epistle to the Romans:

and again Isaiah says,
"The root of Jesse shall come,
the one who rises to rule the Gentiles;
in him the Gentiles shall hope." (15:12)

Who is this "root of Jesse" who would one day rule all the nations of the world? We find the answer if we look closely at the genealogy of Jesus, whose line can be traced…all the way to the great King David, and his father, Jesse (see Matthew 1 and Luke 3). This is the Infant King whose arrival marked the beginning of a new covenant, of which he is the mediator (Hebrews 9:15).

Come Be My Light contains a reflection written by Mother Teresa in which she ponders the humble beginnings of this great king, based on a question Jesus himself raises in Matthew 16:15, "Who do you say that I am?" She replies:

You were born in Bethlehem.
You were wrapped in swaddling clothes by Mary
And put in a manger full of straw.
You were kept warm by the breath of the donkey
That carried Your mother with You in her womb."[37]

For her and for us, the Incarnation was a sign of hope as well as the fulfillment of an ancient prophecy. Despite his meager beginnings, the Son of David and Rod of Jesse has come to earth to be our Eternal King.

A Moment to Reflect

- When you think of Jesus, how do you picture him? As a tiny infant, a preacher in the temple, the miracle worker? Why do you suppose God inspired the writers of the Gospels to take such pains to record Jesus's lineage?
- Take a moment to answer this question Jesus is asking you, "Who do you say that I am?"

A Moment to Pray

O Root of Jesse, the promise of all the ages,
reign in my heart today.

Because of you, I am also the child of your Father,
the King of Heaven and Earth.
Thank you for this unspeakable privilege.
St. Teresa of Calcutta, pray for us!

December 20
O Key of David
Isaiah 7:10–14; Psalm 24-1–6; Luke 1:26–38

O Key of David,
opening the gates of God's eternal Kingdom:
come and free the prisoners of darkness!

In the book of Revelation, we are reminded of this "Key of David" in a message to the church in Philadelphia:

These are the words of the holy one, the true one,
who has the key of David,
who opens and no one will shut,
who shuts and no one opens…

—Revelation 3:7

In the passage that follows, God commends a group of believers who persevered in righteousness despite all odds, despite having little power to effect change in those around them.[38]

Mother Teresa showed a similar sense of determination to follow her "call within a call," even without any visible means of support, when she went out on her own early in her religious life to tend to the needs of the "poorest of the poor" in the streets of Calcutta. In those first few months, Mother Teresa often felt very lonely and overwhelmed by the prospect of the needs of the dozens of children at each school. In desperation, she turned to the Blessed Mother:

> I keep on telling her, "I have no children," just as many years ago she told Jesus, "They have no wine." I put all trust in her Heart. She is sure to give to me in Her own way.[39]

Though Mother Teresa badly needed assistance, other Catholics in the community did not immediately give her their full support. Still, she persevered with faith and trust, and in time she became "mother" to thousands.

If we take a closer look at the story of the Holy Family, we see that even they—in the very center of God's will—had to overcome one challenge after another in order to fulfill the task God gave them to do. He was not born to royalty, but was born in a stable, serenaded by shepherds, fled to Egypt, grew up in obscurity, and suffered a criminal's death after three long years of itinerant preaching. Only in hindsight could his glory be clearly seen.

And so it is for us. We will not fully appreciate the glory in store for us until we are on the other side of heaven's door. In the meantime, our path may take us on puzzling detours. But this Key of David will open that door when our time has come.

A Moment to Reflect

- When have you encountered a situation in which you felt sure you knew the right thing to do—but did not have the support of those "in charge"? What did you learn from this experience?
- What situation of your life will you entrust to the authority and power of God and stop pushing for your own way?

A Moment to Pray

O Key of David,
speak with authority to the hearts of your servant,
that I might rest in confidence and trust.
I know that you can change situations that, humanly speaking,
seem impossible.
St. Teresa of Calcutta, pray for us!

December 21
O RADIANT DAWN
Songs 2:8–14; Psalm 33:2–3, 11–12, 20–21; Luke 1:39–45

O Radiant Dawn,
splendor of eternal light, sun of justice:
come and shine on those who dwell in darkness and in the
shadow of death.

Each time we spend the holidays with my in-laws in Briny Breezes, Florida, we like to head to the beach early Christmas morning to watch the sunrise, breathing deep of the sea air and singing carols. Around six o'clock the first fingers of light creep above the water's edge, finally breaking forth in a most resplendent and radiant dawn.

Of course, as my science-y son reminds us, the *sun* doesn't creep anywhere, not really. Rather, the earth slowly turns toward the light, catching those first rays as it winds around its axis. The "radiant dawn" comes to those who rouse themselves from their soft, warm beds and turn to gaze expectantly toward the light.

In the first chapter of Luke's Gospel, we find that it was the job of John the Baptist to "rouse" the people as they anticipated their own "Radiant Dawn."

By the tender mercy of our God,
    the dawn from on high will break upon us,
to give light to those who sit in darkness and in the shadow of
        death,
    to guide our feet into the way of peace.

—Luke 1:78–79

From his earliest days in the womb of his mother Elizabeth, St. Teresa reminds us, John set about his prophetic task. In recounting the story of the Visitation, she described what happened when the Blessed Mother entered her kinswoman's house: "Just as she entered the house, the little baby John, yet to be born, leapt for joy. It is surprising how God chose a little unborn baby to proclaim the presence of Christ!"[40]

The moment his mother turned toward the Radiant Dawn in Mary's womb, the current of grace flowed through both women. In that moment, every mystery was laid bare through the illumination of their spirits. "How can it be?" no longer mattered as they basked in the wonder of the goodness of the Lord.

A Moment to Reflect

- Remember a time when you struggled to understand something about God and received light from an unexpected place.
- How can you shed a little grace into the life of someone else this week? (If you can't think of a better plan, take your family around for a little Advent caroling.)

A Moment to Pray

O Radiant Dawn,
your light casts out every shadow
whenever I turn toward your light.
Help me never to turn away,
or to be content in darkness.
St. Teresa of Calcutta, pray for us!

December 22
O KING OF ALL NATIONS
1 Samuel 1:24–28; 1 Samuel 2:1–8; Luke 1:46–56

O King of All Nations and keystone of the Church:
come and save man, whom you formed from the dust!

In the summer of 1986, Mother Teresa asked Fidel Castro to allow her to bring her Sisters to Cuba to serve the poor. She was told that the government gives the people what they need. "But the government cannot give love," she gently replied. The Missionaries of Charity were invited to the island nation not long afterward.[41]

Sadly, the government of Albania was not moved by Mother Teresa's appeals when she repeatedly petitioned to be able to see her family. It wasn't until the country opened its doors to the rest of the world that Mother Teresa returned to her homeland in 1990—to visit the grave of her mother and sister. The Egans wrote, "Her personal grief was intensified by the knowledge of the deprivations of the Albanian people and of the persecutions visited on believers in her country [while those doors were closed to her]."[42]

Today's antiphon recollects the "King of All Nations," the righteous ruler who will end all such division and suffering by making a lasting peace between nations, as the prophet Isaiah foretold:

He shall judge between the nations,
and shall arbitrate for many peoples;
they shall beat their swords into plowshares,

and their spears into pruning hooks;
nation shall not lift up sword against nation,
neither shall they learn war any more.

—Isaiah 2:4

The world has not become a more peaceful place since the time of Mother Teresa. Wars and factions, terrorists and tyrants continue to rail against the light. Even within the Church, infighting and conflict belie the fact that the kingdom of God is both already and not yet. And so we continue to wait, echoing the cry of Christians for more than two thousand years, "Maranatha! Come, O King of All the Nations, Come!"

A Moment to Reflect

- What have you heard in the news this week about victims of war and other forms of violence, especially other Christians being persecuted for their faith? Did you remember to pray for them? If not, why not do it now?
- What is one thing you can do to celebrate with your family the "King of All Nations"?

A Moment to Pray

O King of All Nations,
thank you for the many blessings
you have poured out upon my country.
Thank you for the ability to worship you freely and without fear.
Come quickly, Lord Jesus,
so that people all over the world would know and worship you.
St. Teresa of Calcutta, pray for us!

December 23
EMMANUEL
Malachi 3:1–4, 23–24; Psalm 25:4–14; Luke 1:57–66

O Emmanuel, our King and Giver of Law:
come to save us, Lord our God!

Christ's coming into the world as Emmanuel, "God with us," was the ultimate expression of self-giving love—which we, in turn, imitate in order to bring Christ to others. Mother Teresa tells the story of a Hindu gentleman who, when asked what it means to be Christian, gave the simple, surprising answer that a Christian is "someone who gives of himself."

Is this the impression we leave with others, too? That by the power of the God who is with us, we give of ourselves because God first gave himself to us?

In today's antiphon, we welcome "Emmanuel, our King and Giver of the Law." This particular king is not a distant tyrant, demanding tribute from a safe distance. Rather, he comes to his people with an unmistakable sign: "Behold a virgin shall conceive, and bear a son, and his name shall be called Emmanuel" (Isaiah 7:14, DRV).

This Emmanuel, this "God with us" who created the whole universe—including the woman in whose womb he grew—humbled himself so that even the meekest and lowliest of souls could approach him without fear.

The Missionaries of Charity, from the time Mother Teresa was with them to the present, offered this prayer of St. John Newman (d.1890), expressing the hope that they would continue to bring Jesus to those around them in a compelling and irresistible way:

> Dear Jesus, help us to spread your fragrance everywhere we go. Flood our souls with your spirit and life. Penetrate and possess our whole being so utterly that our lives may only be a radiance of yours. Shine through us, and be so in us, that every soul we come in contact with may feel your presence in our soul. Let them look up and see no longer us, but Jesus! Stay with us, and then we shall begin to shine as you shine; so to shine as to be a light to others; the light, O Jesus, will be all from you, none of it will be ours: it will be you shining on others through us. Let us thus praise you in the way you love best by shining on those around us. Let us preach you without preaching, not by words but by our example; by the catching force, the sympathetic influence of what we do, the evident fullness of the love our hearts bear to you. Amen.[44]

A Moment to Reflect

- How have you experienced self-giving love this week? How have you given this kind of love to others?
- How does the way you celebrate Christmas give testimony to the spiritual meaning of the holiday? If a non-Christian neighbor were asked "What is a Christian?" how would this person respond—based on your behavior alone?

A Moment to Pray

O come, O come Emmanuel!
Open my heart to your self-giving love.
Forgive my selfish ways,

and help me to be a reflection of your love in the world.
St. Teresa of Calcutta, pray for us!

December 24

CHRISTMAS EVE

2 Samuel 7:1–16; Psalm 89:2–5, 27–29; Luke 1:67–79

When your days are fulfilled and you lie down with your ancestors, I will raise up your offspring after you, who shall come forth from your body, and I will establish his kingdom. He shall build a house for my name, and I will establish the throne of his kingdom forever. I will be a father to him, and he shall be a son to me.

—2 Samuel 7:12–14

In today's first reading, we anticipate the fulfillment of God's promise to King David. While David had his faults, he was a man after God's own heart, first as a shepherd and then as a king. And so, God made a covenant with David, a promise that his line would produce the long-awaited Messiah who would restore the kingdom of God here on earth.

Like David, this Messiah would be an unlikely king, born in a stable instead of a palace, wielding his authority not as a tyrant, but as God's servant. This reality colors the tribute we offer him, this Son of David we celebrate today. St. Teresa reminds us that Christmas is "a time to welcome Jesus, not in a cold manger of our hearts but in a heart full of love and humility, in a heart so pure, so immaculate, so warm with love for one another."[45]

In Catholic homes across the country, tabletop crèches depicting Mary and Joseph, barnyard animals and shepherds (and the occasional anachronistic wise man) are huddled around an empty manger. Little children scurry to do their chores or make other sweet little sacrifices in order to place a strand of hay in the feedbox where Baby Jesus will miraculously appear on Christmas morning.

The gifts are wrapped. The table is set for company. The stars twinkle overhead, as the world holds its collective breath. *Silent Night, Holy Night.*

Sleep in heavenly peace. And remember, "Keep the joy of loving God in your heart and share this joy with all you meet, especially your family. God bless you, Mother Teresa."[46]

A Moment to Reflect
- As you look back at the story of your life, what have you noticed about the way God keeps his promises with us?
- Consider the "manger of your heart." Is it ready to receive this infant King? Apart from gift-buying and preparing to receive guests, what do you need to do this week to enter into the joy of Christmas?

A Moment to Pray
Heavenly Father,
your ways are so much higher than ours,
with mysteries too great to understand.
Help me to trust you to fulfill your promises
in your time, not mine.
Thank you for the gift of your Son,
the fulfillment of all your promises to us.
St. Teresa of Calcutta, pray for us!

December 25

CHRISTMAS DAY

Isaiah 52:7–10; Psalm 98:1–6; John 1:1–18

How beautiful upon the mountains
   are the feet of the messenger who announces peace,
who brings good news,
   who announces salvation,
   who says to Zion, "Your God reigns."

—Isaiah 52:7

"How beautiful…are the feet." Why do you suppose that this part of the body is so beautiful? Is it because this is the part that moves the messenger to the place where the message is delivered? Or is it because, until they have heard the message, the recipients are bowed so low they cannot raise their eyes any higher, and see only the feet?

As of 1989, St. Teresa was feeding over nine thousand people in Calcutta every day. That many people, in just that one city. If her Sisters didn't cook, the people didn't eat. But they relied on Providence, and God never let them down.

Except, almost, one day. That one day when the Sister in charge came to Mother Teresa to say there was no bread to give the people. The storehouse was empty. What should they do? "I felt numb. It was the first time such a thing had happened," recalled Mother Teresa. What else could they do? They prayed.

That day the city schools closed, and around nine o'clock a bread truck arrived and pulled up to the mission. God would not allow his poor ones to go hungry. They had enough to eat for two days.[47]

For most of us, living this close to the edge of poverty is unthinkable. Our kitchen is so well stocked, especially at this time of year, our biggest concern is how to restrain ourselves from diving face-first into the cookie jar.

And yet, this is also a kind of poverty. Imagine for just a moment what it must have felt like for the Sisters to open their front door…and find their prayers had been answered, that there was now bread enough for *two days!*

When was the last time you were that thankful for small miracles?

A Moment to Reflect

- When was the last time you had to rely on Divine Providence?
- Today is a beautiful day of joyful celebration with friends and family. How will you remember the poor, the lonely, and the hungry?

A Moment to Pray

"Hail and blessed be the hour and moment
in which the Son of God was born of the most pure virgin Mary
at midnight in Bethlehem, in piercing cold.
In that hour vouchsafe, O my God,
to hear our prayers and grant our desires,
through the merits of our savior, Jesus Christ, and his blessed Mother.
Amen."[48]

St. Teresa of Calcutta, pray for us!

Christmas Week through Epiphany

WE WORSHIP THE PRINCE OF PEACE

December 26

When they heard these things, they became enraged and ground their teeth at Stephen. But filled with the Holy Spirit, he gazed into heaven and saw the glory of God and Jesus standing at the right hand of God. "Look," he said, "I see the heavens opened and the Son of Man standing at the right hand of God!" But they covered their ears, and…dragged him out of the city and began to stone him; and the witnesses laid their coats at the feet of a young man named Saul. While they were stoning Stephen, he prayed, "Lord Jesus, receive my spirit."

—Acts 7:54–59

This account from the early Church makes us pause our Christmas celebrations to ponder the story of the first Christian martyr, Stephen. (We also get a glimpse of the Apostle Paul—the young man, Saul). This account of Stephen's death reminds us that the Gospel is not immediately received as good news to all who hear it.

The story reminds us that those who most need to hear the Gospel may be resistant to our efforts as we try to share the love of Christ in our words and with our actions. Are we willing to suffer a little "white martyrdom" in the offhand chance that God is working in that person's heart, below the surface where we cannot see it?

Think of what crossed through Stephen's mind as he looked across the courtyard and saw that young Pharisee, Saul, who was standing with the coats, no doubt scowling at this follower of the Nazarene. As the first rocks hit, did Stephen take a moment to commit Saul's soul, in the same moment he committed his own, into the hands of God?

And what if, in the end, it was that prayer that put the events in motion that culminated on the road to Damascus?

We simply do not know how rich a harvest our small acts of faithfulness will produce. Mother Teresa recalled one "particularly difficult patient" who swore and insulted her as she tried to clean the woman up. Mother Teresa only smiled, and the old woman demanded to know the reason for the smile. "Not everyone behaves like you. Who taught you?"

Kissing the woman on the forehead, the nun replied simply, "My God taught me.... You know my God. My God is called love."[49]

When you are called upon to turn the other cheek, do you remember to turn back with a kiss?

A Moment to Reflect

- Who has been the most exasperating person you encountered this week? How did you respond?
- Do you anticipate that you will encounter any "difficult people" this week? How might you be a sign of love?

A Moment to Pray

Holy Spirit,
you strengthened Stephen as he faced his persecutors,
so that he had courage to persevere in the faith.
Be with me, as I fight my little battles,
that I would persevere as well.
St. Teresa of Calcutta, pray for us!

December 27
FEAST OF ST. JOHN THE EVANGELIST
1 John 1:1–4; Psalm 97:1–12; John 20:1–8

We declare to you what was from the beginning, what we have
heard, what we have seen with our eyes, what we have looked at
and touched with our hands, concerning…the eternal life that
was with the Father and was revealed to us—we declare to you
what we have seen and heard so that you also may have fellow-
ship with us.

—1 John 1:1, 3

One of the gifts I received soon after I became Catholic was a Miraculous
Medal, which, through a series of remarkable events, induced me to set
aside old prejudices about Mary and to use the little sacramental to enrich
my prayer life.

Catholicism is a "touchable" faith. Through her liturgies, sacraments
and sacramentals, and the rich tradition of Catholic art and music, we
experience the richness of her two thousand year history—and encounter
Christ in a personal way, especially through the Eucharist…but also in
each other. As Mother Teresa observed:

Christ became the Bread of Life. But it seems that this act of
self-giving wasn't enough for him. He wanted to give something
more. He wanted to pass on to us the opportunity to give of
ourselves to him, so we could in turn our love for him into living
deeds…. To accomplish that, he became the hungry one, the
naked one, stripped of all earthly goods and comforts…. He will

judge us at the hour of our death…by what we have done, what we have been, to the poor."[50]

According to Tradition, it was St. John the Evangelist to whom the Lord entrusted his mother from the cross in that everlasting exchange: "Woman, here is your son.… Here is your mother" (John 19:26–27). Even in his agony, his first concern was for those he loved most in this world, that they would not be left alone, but would have a tangible reminder of his love for each of them in each other.

And this is precisely the reason why God will not take it kindly when we get to heaven if he finds out we willingly and willfully left someone out in the cold. We were created for connection, created for community. We were created to love.

A Moment to Reflect
- Where did you encounter Christ this week?
- Jesus came to earth to walk among us for a time…and even now, longs to meet us in the Eucharist. Do you have a little time this week to spend some time in Eucharistic adoration?

A Moment to Pray
Dear Jesus,
I do not like to think of you hungry, thirsty, or alone.
Yet you wait for me there in the tabernacle,
hungering and thirsting for a little time with me!
Thank you for the gift of your presence in my life.
St. Teresa of Calcutta, pray for us!

December 28
FEAST OF THE HOLY INNOCENTS
Jeremiah 31:15–17; Revelation 21:1–7

See, the home of God is among mortals.
He will dwell with them as their God;
they will be his peoples,
and God himself will be with them;
he will wipe every tear from their eyes.
Death will be no more;
mourning and crying and pain will be no more,
for the first things have passed away.

—Revelation 21:3–4

Today we remember the young children who were killed by the soldiers under orders of King Herod, who was fearful of the "king of the Jews" of which the Magi had spoken (see Matthew 2:2). Warned in a dream not to return to Herod with their report, the Magi had returned home "by another road" (2:12). Herod was furious that they had eluded him. And all the children under the age of two around Bethlehem paid the ultimate price (2:16).

Now, as then, violence against children continues in dreadful forms, as children die at the hands of their disordered parents from abuse, neglect, and other forms of violence, whether in the womb or in the home. For St. Teresa, violence, like peace, can always be traced to the home.

A mother who is capable of killing her own child only because she is afraid of having another one is poor indeed!... Nevertheless, we read in Scripture, "Even if a mother should forsake her child, I will not forsake you. I have you in the palm of my hand."

If a mother can kill her own child, how long will it be before we start to kill one another? We should not be surprised when we hear about murders, deaths, wars, and hate in the world today.... Let's go with our Lady to search out that child and take him or her home.[51]

If as a society we cannot find a way to protect these innocent ones, not just in the womb but throughout their formative years, we cannot feign surprise when these innocents fail to meet their God-given potential or go on to repeat the cycle of neglect and abuse themselves.

"Bring the child to me. Give me the child," Mother Teresa would plead with the at-risk mothers. What is God asking you to do?

A Moment to Reflect

- What episodes of violence have you seen in the news this week that could be directly traced to childhood abuse and neglect? What did you do to help make the world a more peaceful place?
- What one thing could you do to help a struggling family in your community?

A Moment to Pray

Holy Spirit,
you are everywhere, you see everything—
behind closed doors, curtained and barred windows,
even inside prison walls.
Make me aware of the misery of others,

and show me how I can alleviate their suffering
out of love for Christ.
St. Teresa of Calcutta, pray for us!

December 29

JOYFUL SUFFERING

1 John 2:3–11; Psalm 96:1–6; Luke 2:22–35

> Now there was a man in Jerusalem whose name was Simeon; this man was righteous and devout, looking forward to the consolation of Israel, and the Holy Spirit rested on him. It had been revealed to him by the Holy Spirit that he would not see death before he had seen the Lord's Messiah.
>
> —Luke 2:25–26

When Jesus was forty days old, Joseph and Mary brought their son to present him at the Temple and to make a sacrifice on his behalf. It was there they encountered two holy souls, Simeon and Anna, who had long awaited the promised Messiah. "Guided by the Spirit" (v. 27), first Simeon then Anna recognized Jesus for who he was: God's promise fulfilled.

Although it was a moment of great joy, that joy was also tinged with sadness as Simeon predicted that this small child was a sign of the "falling and rising of many in Israel" and that a sword would one day pierce Mary's heart (v. 35). Even for the Holy Family, life would not be one continuous party, but a study in contrasts: joy and sorrow, pain and pleasure, shadow and light.

Even in moments of great contentment, they lived with the knowledge of certain suffering ahead. How, then, could "Our Lady of Sorrows" also be "Cause of Our Joy"? Because of the great love in her heart. St. Teresa tells us:

True love causes pain. Jesus, in order to give us the proof of his love, died on the cross. A mother, in order to give birth to her baby, has to suffer. If you really love one another, you will not be able to avoid making sacrifices.[52]

Within the vocation of marriage there are almost limitless opportunities for this kind of joyful sacrifice. Well, sometimes joyful—other times more reluctant, but resigned. The spouse who must accept the cross of a spouse's infertility; the parent who discovers a child is not as "perfect" as was hoped; the mental illness that threatens to destroy both spouses; the friend who is not as constant as you had once believed. Momentary joys can never entirely displace the shadows.

And yet, we are called to joy. Even as the sword pierces our hearts, we remain standing in the hope of redemption. We, too, can anticipate our consolation.

A Moment to Reflect
- Recall a time when love caused you great suffering. When we offer those sufferings back to God, he makes our hearts grow in compassion.
- Do you know someone who is suffering joyfully for Christ? Why not drop that person a note of encouragement?

A Moment to Pray
Lord Jesus,
even you were not immune to the pangs of pain and loss,
for you embraced the whole human experience—yet without sin.
Give me strength not just to endure,
but to "offer it up" with joy.
St. Teresa of Calcutta, pray for us!

Sunday between Christmas and January 1
(December 30 if January 1 is a Sunday)
FEAST OF THE HOLY FAMILY
Sirach 3:2–6, 12–14; Psalm 128:1–5; Luke 2:41–52

Now every year his parents went to Jerusalem for the festival of the Passover. And when he was twelve years old, they went up as usual for the festival. When the festival was ended and they started to return, the boy Jesus stayed behind in Jerusalem, but his parents did not know it.

—Luke 2:41–43

Any parent who has ever momentarily lost sight of a child at the grocery store or in the mall will appreciate the dry-throated panic that must have hit Joseph and Mary when they discovered their Son was missing from their traveling party on the way home from Jerusalem. True, the city had been full of devout pilgrims…but also far more nefarious characters who were seeking to defraud and, if necessary, take by force the wealth that had poured into the city in massive caravans.

Mary was the perfect mother—and yet, like Jesus, she must have experienced the whole range of human emotion, even as she submitted herself entirely to the will of her Son's Father through her tears.

Joseph was a devout man—yet, like any man, would gladly have walked through fire rather than face the tears of his wife. He was likely most animated and highly motivated in the search.

"Jesus, where are you?"

The question rang out through the city streets until it became a whispery echo, reminiscent of another time and place, when a Father went in search of his son. "But the LORD God called to the man [Adam], and said to him, "Where are you?" (Genesis 3:9).

One thing was for certain: The New Adam was not in the garden. Not yet.

A Moment to Reflect

- Think about some of the family-related challenges you have faced this week. Do you think Mary and Joseph encountered similar challenges—and might they have dealt with those challenges a bit differently?
- Today's reflection question comes from St. Teresa: "If Mary and Joseph were looking for a place to make a home for Jesus, would they choose your home?"[53]

A Moment to Pray

Lord Jesus,
though you had the perfect parents,
and were yourself the perfect child,
still your Sacred Heart has room to store
the many intentions of parents who struggle.
Give me the strength and courage I need
to fulfill the task you have given me to do.
St. Teresa of Calcutta, pray for us!

December 30
JOSEPH'S DREAM
1 John 1:5–2:2; Psalm 124:2–8; Matthew 2:13–18

Now after they had left, an angel of the Lord appeared to Joseph in a dream and said, "Get up, take the child and his mother, and flee to Egypt, and remain there until I tell you; for Herod is about to search for the child, to destroy him." Then Joseph got up, took the child and his mother by night, and went to Egypt, and remained there until the death of Herod. This was to fulfill what had been spoken by the Lord through the prophet, "Out of Egypt I have called my son."

—Matthew 2:13–15

Talk about night terrors. With a dream like that, it's no wonder that Joseph sprang to life in the dead of night, intent on getting his family to safety as quickly as possible.

Because he was a man of deep prayer as well as a man of action, he was able to heed the warning and escape from the murderous hoards. Through prayer and action, he expressed his love for God, and for his family. The two were intimately connected, as Mother Teresa observed:

Our work is the fruit of our prayer, so that if our work is not going well, we must examine our prayer life. If we neglect our work or are harsh, proud, moody, and angry, then we should examine our prayer life.[54]

How would you describe your prayer life right now? Hit-or-miss? Five minutes every morning? Do you try to take a moment at the end of the day to thank God for the ways you experienced his presence throughout the day and ask him to go before you as you face tomorrow's challenges?

If you had been the one to receive such a vision in the middle of the night, what do you think your response might have been? Would you have been as certain as Joseph was that it was God who was speaking?

And if not, what are you prepared to do to change this?

A Moment to Reflect

- Has your work been the fruit of prayer, or have you found yourself wrestling with harshness, resentment, and anger?
- As the new year approaches, think about whether you need to cultivate more regular, persistent prayer habits. When is the best time for you to pray for the work of your day?

A Moment to Pray

Heavenly Father,
you gave us work to do
from the earliest days in the Garden of Eden.
Prayer and work, "*Ora et labora*,"
has been the theme of all Christian living.
Help me to stay close to you throughout the day,
and to hear your voice as I work.
St. Teresa of Calcutta, pray for us!

December 31
NEW YEAR'S EVE
1 John 2:18–21; Psalm 96:1–13; John 1:1–18

In the beginning was the Word, and the Word was with God, and the Word was God.... He was in the world, and the world came into being through him; yet the world did not know him. He came to what was his own, and his own people did not accept him. But to all who received him, who believed in his name, he gave power to become children of God.

—John 1:1, 10–12

When we first became foster parents to a sibling group of three, our first foster son would spend hours under a small table in the family room, hiding from my husband. Ever the gentle giant, Craig would try to coax the three-year-old out with a bowl of Cheetos, the little boy's favorite snack. The child would emerge briefly, grab a handful, and run for cover. It wasn't until Craig got down on all fours and started playing "Daddy Monster" with another child that the boy (now our son) overcame his fears about the "big man" and joined in the game.

In today's reading we find that, just as my husband made himself small to help that terrified toddler learn to trust, God made himself small in order to reach us. Sadly, even this does not turn every heart toward him. Blinded by selfishness and pride, many refuse to surrender even to this benevolent force of love. Jesus was rejected even from the moment of his birth, as St. Teresa tells us:

Each time Jesus wanted to prove his love for us, he was rejected by mankind. Before his birth his parents asked for a simple dwelling place and there was none because his parents were poor. The innkeeper looked at the poor dress of Joseph the carpenter, thinking that he will not be able to pay, and he was refused. But Mother Earth opened its cave and took in the Son of God.[55]

This short reflection is a wonderful reminder that God doesn't always speak to us through the Bible, or through other people. Sometimes he whispers to us through the pines, or shouts his glory through the ocean spray. He speaks in the language our hearts are most likely to hear.

No matter the language, the message is the same: Can you find a place for the Christ Child in your heart and home today?

A Moment to Reflect

- Did you encounter someone who is stubbornly refusing to consider the truth of the Gospel? Pray that the Holy Spirit would soften this person's heart.
- Take some time to play like a kid again, and think about the fact that you are truly a child of God.

A Moment to Pray

Heavenly Father,
thank you for sending your Son into the world
to show me how much you love me
and want me to be part of your family.
Help me to live so the whole world
sees the family resemblance.
St. Teresa of Calcutta, pray for us!

January 1
SOLEMNITY OF MARY, MOTHER OF GOD
Numbers 6:22–27; Psalm 67:2–8; Galatians 4:4–7; Luke 2:16–21

So they went with haste and found Mary and Joseph, and the child lying in the manger. When they saw this, they made known what had been told them about this child; and all who heard it were amazed at what the shepherds told them. But Mary treasured all these words and pondered them in her heart. The shepherds returned, glorifying and praising God for all they had heard and seen, as it had been told them.

—Luke 2:16–20

As the Mother of God, Mary had a front-row seat to many miraculous events. First the angel, then the shepherds and the Magi, then the many miracles Jesus worked in the course of his earthly ministry. His resurrection, ascension to heaven, and Pentecost. She was witness to all of it, and the graces that flowed through her then continue to flow even to this day and age as she continues to work miracles on behalf of all her children.

When St. Teresa needed to build a motherhouse for her Missionaries of Charity, she promised the Blessed Mother 85,000 Memorares to secure this miracle for her ministry. With a great sense of urgency, the Sisters began to make good on Mother Teresa's promise:

Remember, O most gracious Virgin Mary,
that never was it known that anyone who fled to your protection,
implored your help, or sought your intercession,

was left unaided.
Inspired by this confidence,
I fly to you, O Virgin of virgins, my Mother.
To you do I come, before you I stand, sinful and sorrowful.
O Mother of the Word Incarnate,
despise not my petitions,
but in your mercy, hear and answer me.
Amen.

Counting noses, Mother Teresa did some quick calculations and realized that she and her Sisters would each need to offer the prayer *many* times before they would reach 85,000 prayers. So she gathered the children from Shishu Bhavan and the sick ones from Nirmal Hriday and taught them the prayer as well. "The building did not take long to become ours," Mother said.[56]

Does it surprise you that someone as holy as Mother Teresa would attempt to force the hand of the Blessed Mother in this way, by "nagging" her with petitions? I suppose if this were the only time Mother Teresa had cast herself upon Our Lady's favor in this way, it is possible the outcome would have been very different.

Intercession is like any other form of communication: The intimacy of the relationship can greatly affect the way the message is perceived. It is no wonder, then, that so devoted a daughter as Mother Teresa would have turned Our Lady's head…or that Mother Teresa had such confidence that the Blessed Mother would hear her.

What does this say to you about the secret of catching the ear of the Blessed Mother?

A Moment to Reflect

- Did you ask Mary to help you this week? How could she help you now?
- The world is full of small miracles if we take the time to look. This week, be open to the hand of God in your life, and thank him for the small miracles you encounter each day.

A Moment to Pray

Mother Mary,
you took time to ponder all the wonderful things
you heard and saw as the mother of Jesus.
Help me to be more mindful of the small miracles around me,
and to ponder these signs of God's presence in the world each day.
St. Teresa of Calcutta, pray for us!

January 2
SONG OF A GENEROUS HEART
1 John 2:22–28; Psalm 98:1–4; John 1:19–28

All the ends of the earth have seen
the victory of our God.
Make a joyful noise to the Lord, all the earth;
break forth into joyous song and sing praises.

—Psalm 98:4

"Sing to the Lord a new song," begins Psalm 98. With the New Year comes a fresh opportunity to praise God for his goodness to us and another invitation to imitate, even in a small way, his generosity to his children.

Some people spend a lifetime waiting for the "right time" to be generous. We are happy to give what we no longer need but find it hard to make a truly sacrificial gift. College and retirement funds, vacation savings, and safety "cushions" are all good things. But do these things justify our turning a blind eye to the one who is in immediate need?

St. Teresa would frequently challenge her benefactors in the West not simply to give from their surplus but to give of themselves. "I don't want you to give to us from your abundance. I don't need money from your abundance.… I ask that you lend your hands in understanding."[57]

Upon first reading this line, I wondered about it. Didn't the poor benefit more if someone dug into deep pockets and pulled out a substantial gift than if an empathetic soul offered a widow's mite?

And yet, like any good mother, St. Teresa was looking to the needs of both children—the physically impoverished of the East and the spiritually impoverished (but significantly more affluent) devotees of the West. We cannot eradicate our own poverty by relieving someone else's. But when we reach out with our humanity, rather than our checkbook, the healing graces flow in both directions.

As you begin this year, perhaps your resolutions are already fading from memory. Still, the Lord invites us to "sing a new song," to praise him not only with our lips, but with our deeds.

A Moment to Reflect

- Jesus said, "For where your treasure is, there your heart will be also" (Luke 12:34). What does your checkbook say about where your heart is this week?

- How can you be more generous with your time and treasure this week?

A Moment to Pray

Heavenly Father,
you have given me so much to be thankful for
[name some of those blessings here].
I recognize that these blessings are not intended for me alone.
Help me to recognize and respond
when I see a need that I can fill today.
St. Teresa of Calcutta, pray for us!

ВНИМАНИЕ

January 3
GOD HAS NO "ONLY CHILD"
1 John 2:29–3:6; Psalm 98:1–6; John 1:29–34

> See what love the Father has given us, that we should be called
> children of God; and that is what we are. The reason the world
> does not know us is that it did not know him. Beloved, we are
> God's children now; what we will be has not yet been revealed.
> What we do know is this: when he is revealed, we will be like
> him, for we will see him as he is. And all who have this hope in
> him purify themselves, just as he is pure.
>
> —1 John 3:1–3

When people look at my daughter, they frequently comment on how
much she looks like me—despite the fact that we share no biological
connection. More than a decade of life has passed between us, and over
time we have acquired each other's little quirks and idiosyncrasies, just as
loving married couples often do. Over time, love leaves a luster as unique
as a fingerprint.

The same is true, or can be, with the family of God. Just as it was the
Blessed Mother who gave Jesus the shape of his jaw, the color of his eyes,
the texture of his hair, so she gives to us, her children, a kind of spiritual
likeness the more we strive to imitate her in love. Similarly, our Heavenly
Father pours his love and mercy upon us as his children by adoption
(Galatians 4:5; Ephesians 1:5). And in his doing so, we begin to take on
that luster of love that gradually restores in us that image that he created

us to bear, not just individually, but as the Bride of Christ, members of his Body, the Church.

St. Teresa reminds us of how much we depend on one another as we make our way toward heaven. As we make the journey, none of us will get very far alone.

> The Holy Family consisted of Jesus, Mary and Joseph, not just Jesus alone. For the family to be complete, it was necessary to have Joseph the carpenter alongside the greatness of Jesus and the spotlessness of Mary. So too, in our churches, several people may be very capable but they do not make up the community. We need others to complete the team.[58]

A Moment to Reflect

- What special memory of your faith community will you carry with you into the New Year?
- How will you continue to celebrate this Divine Infant and his Mother and keep them at the center of your home?

A Moment to Pray

Thank you, Father God,

for the brothers and sisters you have put on my path,

children who delight your heart.

Help us to love and serve each other,

so that we might look more and more like you.

St. Teresa of Calcutta, pray for us!

January 4
CHILDREN OF GOD
1 John 3:7–10; Psalm 98:1–9; John 1:35–42

The children of God and the children of the devil are revealed in
this way: all who do not do what is right are not from God, nor
are those who do not love their brothers and sisters.

—1 John 3:10

In the Gospels, Jesus reserved some of his strongest denunciations for the
Pharisees—the Jewish leaders of his day. "You brood of vipers!" (Matthew
3:7), he called them, calling his followers not to follow in the footsteps of
those who would "tie up heavy burdens, hard to bear, and lay them on the
shoulders of others; but they themselves are unwilling to lift a finger to
move them" (Matthew 23:4–5).[59]

It is a regrettable flaw in human nature, the tendency to build walls
instead of bridges, to become complacent and unwilling to look beyond
our own immediate circle to decide whom we will help or accept. Mother
Teresa, on the other hand, loved across the cultural and religious bound-
aries and inspired others to do the same.

One night upon sitting down to supper, Mother Teresa learned that a
nearby Hindu family with eight children had not eaten in days. She and
her Sisters promptly wrapped up the rice from their own supper and went
to the family, who received it gratefully. The mother then divided the
rice and disappeared. It seemed the large Muslim family next door was
hungry, too.

Mother recalls that they did not bring the family more rice that night, "I wanted them to experience the joy of loving and sharing. You should have seen the faces of those little children! They barely understood what their mother had done, yet their eyes shined with a smile."[60]

Reading this story, the question naturally arises: Do I know any families who do not know Jesus, well enough to know of a need that I could fill? How am I adding to the burden and shame of poverty by my own thoughtlessness? Am I truly a child of God—or a Pharisee?

A Moment to Reflect

- Where might you be most likely to meet someone whose burden you might lift a little? When were you last there? When might you go again?
- How might you live more intentionally as a "child of God" in the coming week?

A Moment to Pray

Lord, I do not want to be a Pharisee, placing unnecessary burdens of judgment and shame on those around me. Show me how to lift up my brothers and sisters, especially those who most need to know you. St. Teresa of Calcutta, pray for us!

January 5
JESUS, DO YOU SEE ME?
1 John 3:11–21; Psalm 100:1–5; John 1:43–51

When Jesus saw Nathanael coming toward him, he said of him, "Here is truly an Israelite in whom there is no deceit!" Nathanael asked him, "Where did you get to know me?" Jesus answered, "I saw you under the fig tree before Philip called you." Nathanael replied, "Rabbi, you are the Son of God! You are the King of Israel!" Jesus answered, "Do you believe because I told you that I saw you under the fig tree? You will see greater things than these."

—John 1:47–50

One Heart Full of Love recounts a story of Mother Teresa's in which she meets an Aborigine in Australia. The man lived in squalor, but upon entering his house, Mother Teresa noticed a beautiful lamp that had obviously not been used for a long time. She asked him whether he lit the lamp, and the man replied, "For whom? No one ever comes to my house. I spend days without seeing a human face. I have no need to light the lamp."

Mother asked if he would light the lamp if her Sisters came to visit him every evening, and the man agreed. Writes Mother Teresa, "The sisters made it their habit to visit him every evening. The old man began to light the lamp for them and to keep it clean. He began to keep his house clean, too. He lived for two more years…. [Visiting him] was a very small thing, but in that dark loneliness a light was lit and continued to shine."

Some people go through life feeling invisible. Very often such people do not need a hand-out nearly as much as they need to be noticed, their human dignity acknowledged and respected not because of what they contribute, but simply because they are souls God loves.

To be sure, these individuals are not always the easiest to love—the obnoxious child, critical parent, guarded neighbor, back-biting coworker. Nathanael must have rubbed Jesus the wrong way when he heard Nathanael's retort, "Can anything good come out of Nazareth?" (v. 46). But where some would have seen rudeness, Jesus saw honesty. And where some would have seen squalor, Mother Teresa saw the lamp.

A Moment to Reflect

- What are some of the moments this week that you would have been a little embarrassed if Jesus told you he had been watching from a distance. What loving word would he have used to describe you?
- Who is the "Nathanael" who needs a bit of kindness and understanding from you?

A Moment to Pray

St. Teresa,
you looked into the eyes of the most marginalized souls
and saw not just potential,
but Jesus "in distressing disguise."
Pray for me today,
that I might be ever mindful of Jesus's eyes upon me,
loving me not for what I do,
but for who he created me to be.
St. Teresa of Calcutta, pray for us!

Sunday after January 1
(Traditional date: January 6)
SOLEMNITY OF THE EPIPHANY
Isaiah 60:1–6; Psalm 72:1–13; Matthew 2:1–12

When they had heard the king, they set out; and there, ahead of them, went the star that they had seen at its rising, until it stopped over the place where the child was. When they saw that the star had stopped, they were overwhelmed with joy. On entering the house, they saw the child with Mary his mother; and they knelt down and paid him homage. Then, opening their treasure chests, they offered him gifts of gold, frankincense, and myrrh.

—Matthew 2:9–11

Every baby who comes into the world arrives with just three things: a gift to share, a burden to carry, and a job to do. Once you've done your job as best you can, out of love for God, he calls you back to heaven to be with him forever. Each person's job—like his gifts and burdens—is different, something only he can do, and only when the time is right.

After the Magi leave their gifts with the Holy Family, Scripture is silent about what became of them other than they returned home "by another road." (According to some, their remains were discovered by St. Helena in the fifth century and were eventually transferred to the cathedral of Cologne in the twelfth century.[61]) And yet, the timely gifts of those kings may have provided the resources the Holy Family needed to save the little Christ Child from the clutches of King Herod.

And yet, the most beautiful gift we can offer to God, says St. Teresa, is not something money can buy: "We must grow in a clear conviction of our duty to be holy as Jesus is holy. Holiness is one of the most beautiful gifts a human heart can offer to God."[62]

A Moment to Reflect

- What gift has God given to you to share with the rest of the world?
- What burden have you been carrying, to keep you close to God?
- How can you encourage others this week to share their gifts at home, in your parish, or in your community—and in so doing, bring the joy of Jesus wherever you may go?

A Moment to Pray

St. Teresa of Calcutta

You allowed the thirsting love of Jesus on the Cross

To become a living flame within you,

And so became the light of his love to all.

Obtain from the Heart of Jesus (here make your request).

Teach me to allow Jesus to penetrate and possess my whole being so completely

That my life, too, may radiate his light and love to others. Amen.

Immaculate Heart of Mary, Cause of Our Joy, pray for us.

St. Teresa of Calcutta, pray for us.[63]

Feast of the Baptism of the Lord
IN THE SILENCE OF THE HEART
Isaiah 42:1–7; Psalm 29:1–10; Acts 10:34–38; Matthew 3:13–17

And when Jesus had been baptized, just as he came up from the water, suddenly the heavens were opened to him and he saw the Spirit of God descending like a dove and alighting on him. And a voice from heaven said, "This is my Son, the Beloved, with whom I am well pleased."

—Matthew 3:16–17

In today's Gospel we read of the first of two important moments in the life of Christ prior to his public ministry. First, he assents to John's baptism; then, he comes out of the water and is driven into the desert for forty days. This latter experience is the basis of Lent, the forty-day journey to Easter.

This surrender to the heights and depths is seen again and again in the lives of saints. Consolation and desolation alike are part of the journey. Despite her passionate love for Jesus, Mother Teresa also experienced years of interior darkness, in which she could not sense the presence of the one she loved most. So how did she carry on? How did she continue in her ministry, continue to pray when she felt as though her prayers were merely bouncing off the ceiling? In a speech in Berlin on June 8, 1980, Mother Teresa offered these reassuring words to those who find it hard to pray:

Prayer is not meant…to trouble us. It is something to look forward to, to talk to my Father, to talk to Jesus…. And when the times come when we can't pray, it is very simple: if Jesus is in my heart, let him pray, let me allow Him to pray in me, to talk to His Father in the silence of my heart.[64]

A Moment to Reflect

- Think about the high and low moments of your life. When was the last time God felt very near to you—or very far away?
- Now take a moment to think about what God has in store as you move into Ordinary Time. These water and desert experiences were merely moments of preparation. What do you sense God has been saying to you as you've been reading this? Is he preparing you for some change ahead? If you're not sure, why not ask?

A Moment to Pray

Jesus, I trust in you!
At baptism, at confirmation, and especially in the Eucharist
you come to me, strengthening me for the journey ahead.
I do not know what is in store for me in the coming year,
but I offer you my "yes," the gift you want most.
Thank you for your guidance, your protection, and your love.
St. Teresa of Calcutta, pray for us!

Feast Days and Other Special Days
during Advent and Christmas

December 6

FEAST OF ST. NICHOLAS
Isaiah 6:1–8; Psalm 40:2–11; Luke 10:1–9

Then one of the seraphs flew to me, holding a live coal that had been taken from the altar with a pair of tongs. The seraph touched my mouth with it and said: "Now that this has touched your lips, your guilt has departed and your sin is blotted out." Then I heard the voice of the Lord saying, "Whom shall I send, and who will go for us?" And I said, "Here am I; send me!

—Isaiah 6:6–8

St. Nicholas and St. Teresa could well be considered kindred spirits. Both were raised in devout Christian families, and both spent much of their lives and personal resources tending to the needs of the poor, the sick, and the suffering. And both had almost unlimited compassion for children in dire circumstances.

Born in the fourth century, St. Nicholas (also known as the "Bishop of Myra" and "Nicholas the Wonderworker") was among those persecuted under Diocletian, Many miracles were attributed to him after his death, including several touching stories in which he rescues abducted or lost children.

Similarly, St. Teresa spent much of her time and energy tending to the needs of young children and her efforts to find good families and homes for the orphans. Early in her ministry, she found that Indian families were often unwilling to take in many of these children—especially girls, who were considered a liability since they would one day belong to their husband's family, unable to tend to their own elderly parents.

Over time, however, the Missionaries of Charity saw this change. Observed one Sister: "Some years ago, people wanted only boys and were fussy about light skins and nice noses. People are now increasingly prepared to accept children virtually unseen, even girls." Mother Teresa agreed. "Every day we have one or two families, even high-caste Hindu families, who come to adopt a child."[65]

A Moment to Reflect

- Have you ever considered foster parenting, adoption, or sponsoring a child in need? Can you ask someone who is currently doing one of these things about the process in order to make an informed decision?
- Ask God if he wants you to do something specific to help a child—or to encourage another family who has already responded to this call.

A Moment to Pray

Father God,
give me your heart for the world.
Help me, like St. Nicholas,
show love and compassion
for the children who cross my path,
and to respond to their needs with a generous heart.
St. Teresa of Calcutta, pray for us!

December 8

> In Christ we have also obtained an inheritance, having been destined according to the purpose of him who accomplishes all things according to his counsel and will, so that we, who were the first to set our hope on Christ, might live for the praise of his glory.
>
> —Ephesians 1:11–12

When I was a new Catholic, I remember hearing the term "Immaculate Conception" for the first time and imagining Mary serenely attending to her household chores, washing the dishes and sweeping the floors until no speck of dirt remained and finding the angel in the dustbin, ready to spring the news on her that she was about to become a mother.

With some relief, I discovered I was not alone in my misunderstanding. However, as my sponsor soon informed me with an admirably straight face, this feast actually commemorates the conception of *Mary*, not Jesus. This important Marian dogma was promulgated by Pope Pius IX in 1854, affirming the long-standing teaching of the Church about how *Mary* was "from the first moment of her conception… preserved immune from all stain of original sin" (*CCC* 491).[66]

As the Ark of the New Covenant that contained the "Bread of Life," Mary was preserved by God from both original and personal sin because of the special role she was to fulfill. Consecrated to the Lord from a tender age, she was later entrusted into the tender care and protection of Joseph—who knew full well that she belonged to God alone. And from the cross, Jesus gave his mother her final consecration, to be mother of all the faithful (see John 19:27), drawing all of us closer to her beloved Son. St. Teresa writes:

> On this feast of the Immaculate Conception, let us consecrate our lives to Mary.... How clean our words must be to be able to proclaim the good news to the poor. Mary, the most pure virgin, will teach us to be pure so that when the poor look at us they see only Jesus.[67]

Now, my home will never be immaculate enough to impress anyone with my housekeeping skills. But I take some comfort in knowing that I have a heavenly mother who patiently watches over me and loves me even when her "problem child" falls short of the mark. Don't you?

A Moment to Reflect

- How would you describe your relationship with Mary? Can you recall ever praying to her or asking for her help? She wants to hear from you!
- If you have never consecrated yourself or your household to Mary, consider getting more information about this, such as Michael Gaitley's *33 Days to Morning Glory,* to see if this is something you would like to do.

A Moment to Pray

Immaculate Heart of Mary, our Queen and Mother, be more and more our way to Jesus, the light of Jesus, and the life of Jesus in each one of us. In return for this gift, let us be more and more a cause of joy to one another, the way of peace to one another and the living of love of Jesus for one another. [68]

St. Teresa of Calcutta, pray for us!

December 12
FEAST OF OUR LADY OF GUADALUPE
Zechariah 2:10–13; Judith 13:18–19; Luke 1:26–38

Sing and rejoice, O daughter Zion! For lo, I will come and dwell in your midst, says the LORD. Many nations shall join themselves to the LORD on that day, and shall be my people; and I will dwell in your midst. And you shall know that the LORD of hosts has sent me to you.

—Zechariah 2:10–11

In the story of St. Juan Diego and Our Lady of Guadalupe, the poor farmer is given an impossible task: to persuade the bishop that the Blessed Mother wanted a chapel built for her, there on the Hill of Tepeyac. Juan Diego and his wife had been among the first to be baptized by the Franciscan missionaries who had arrived in Mexico in 1524. He was a man of faith and yet, he was just a poor farmer. Why on earth would the Blessed Mother appear to *him*?

Why, indeed. "Am I not here, I who am your mother?" the woman, dressed like an Aztec princess, asked the sheepish Juan Diego, who had hurried past their appointed meeting place to attend to his dying uncle. Reluctantly, he gathered into his tilma the roses that had miraculously bloomed by the roadside, took them to the bishop. And soon her chapel was built, just as Our Lady had asked.

How often are we skeptical when it comes to lending a hand to one of God's "poor ones"? How often do we make them prove they are worthy of our assistance? St. Teresa tells of a woman who came to her, begging for food for her child, who had been turned away in several other places and told to work for what she needed. The nun gave her food but it was too late, and the child had died of hunger. St. Teresa concludes: "We will not have them tomorrow if we do not feed them today. So be concerned about what you can do today."[69]

A Moment to Reflect

- In many of the apparitions of the Blessed Mother, in all parts of the world, she comes not to the religious elite but to the poor and humble, or to children. Why do you think that is so?
- The Blessed Mother has appeared all over the world and assumes many different titles and appearances to God's children. How many of them can you think of—and which is your favorite, and why?

A Moment to Pray

Our Lady of Guadalupe,
you appeared to Juan Diego
in order to make your Son known
to the poor and humble native races of Mexico
—appearing not as an outsider or oppressor,
but as one of them.
Help me so to identify
with those I try to help in your name.
St. Teresa of Calcutta, pray for us!

Notes

1. Lavonne Neff, *A Life for God: The Mother Teresa Reader* (Ann Arbor, MI: Charis, 1995), 105.
2. Brian Kolodiejchuk, MC, *Mother Teresa: Come Be My Light: The Private Writings of the Saint of Calcutta* (New York: Doubleday, 2007), vii.
3. Subrata Nagchoudhury, "Missionaries of Charity: What after Nirmala?" *The Indian Express,* June 15, 2015.
4. Bishop Robert Barron, "Saint of Light, Saint of Darkness," Aleteia. http://aleteia.org/2016/01/06/ saint-of-light-saint-of-darkness. Accessed March 29, 2016.
5. Navin Chawla, *Mother Teresa: The Authorized Biography* (Rockport, MA: Element, 1992), 97.
6. Chawla, 218.
7. Chawla, xv.
8. Mother Teresa, *One Heart Full of Love.* José Luis Gonzalez-Balado, ed. (Cincinnati: Servant, 1988), 135.
9. Mother Teresa, *One Heart Full of Love,* 98.
10. Mother Teresa, *One Heart Full of Love,* 98.
11. Kathryn Spink, *Mother Teresa: A Complete Authorized Biography* (San Francisco: HarperSanFrancisco, 1997), 86.
12. Spink, 255.
13. Mother Teresa, *One Heart Full of Love,* 37.
14. From an address at the National Prayer Breakfast, February 3, 1994. EWTN library.
15. Mother Teresa, *Thirsting for God.* Angelo Scolozzi, ed. (Cincinnati: Servant, 2013), 107.
16. Malcolm Muggeridge, *Something Beautiful for God* (San Francisco: Harper & Row, 1971), 119.

17. Eileen Egan and Kathleen Egan, OSB, *Suffering into Joy: What Mother Teresa Teaches about True Joy* (Ann Arbor, MI: Servant, 1994), 67.

18. Mother Teresa, *Thirsting for God,* 142.

19. Mother Teresa, as quoted in "I Thirst for You Prayer" by the Missionaries of Charity Fathers. http: / / www.mcpriests.com / 03_I_thirst_PrayerEN.htm. Accessed February 15, 2016. [BAD LINK]

20. Spink, 152.

21. Mother Teresa, *Thirsting for God,* 169.

22. Mother Teresa, *Thirsting for God*, 87.

23. Mother Teresa, *Thirsting for God,* 21.

24. Egan and Egan, 78.

25. Mother Teresa, *Thirsting for God,* 185.

26. Charles Austin Miles, "In the Garden" (New York: RCA Victor, 1912).

27. *Mother Teresa: Her Essential Wisdom.* Carol Kelly-Gangi, ed. (New York: Fall River, 2006), 30.

28. Pope Francis, *Laudato Si* (On Care for Our Common Home), 204.

29. Egan and Egan, 74.

30. Mother Teresa, *One Heart Full of Love,* 51.

31. Kelly-Gangi, 57.

32. Note: The "O Antiphons" are read in the final week of Advent before Christmas, from December 17 through December 23. Because Christmas is a moveable feast, and the antiphons fall on specific dates, they may begin during the Third Week of Advent. The Fourth Sunday of Advent will replace one of these dates in any year. The Antiphons for this section are from the USCCB website: http: / / www.usccb.org / prayer-and-worship / prayers-and-devotions / prayers / the-o-antiphons-of-advent.cfm.

33. Desmond Doig, *Mother Teresa: Her People and Work* (New York: Nachiketa, 1976), 107.

34. Pope John Paul II, *Beatification of Mother Teresa of Calcutta: Homily of His Holiness John Paul II.* World Mission Sunday, 4.

35. Mother Teresa, *Total Surrender.* Angelo Scolozzi, ed. (Ann Arbor, MI: Servant, 1985), 76.

36. From the traditional hymn "O Come, O Come, Emmanuel." Translated into English from an eighth-century poem by John Mason Neale in 1851.

37. The "stem" is alternately referred to as a "root" or "shoot" in some translations. The genealogies of both Mary and Joseph can be traced back to the lineage of King David, the son of Jesse. The genealogy of Mary is found in the Gospel of Matthew 1:1–17. The genealogy of Joseph, Jesus's legal or adoptive father, is found in Luke 3:23–38.

38. Kolodiejchuk, 302.

39. See Revelation 3:8–13; Isaiah 22:22.

40. Chawla, 42.

41. Mother Teresa, *One Heart Full of Love*, 137.

42. Egan and Egan, 34.

43. Egan and Egan, 68.

44. Mother Teresa, *Thirsting for God*, 208.

45. Spink, 205.

46. Chawla, 196.

47. Egan and Egan, 81.

48. Traditional Advent Novena prayer.

49. David Scott, *A Revolution of Love: The Meaning of Mother Teresa* (Chicago: Loyola, 2005), 16.

50. Mother Teresa, *One Heart Full of Love,* 3.

51. Mother Teresa, *One Heart Full of Love,* 41.

52. José Luis Gonzalez-Balado, ed. *Mother Teresa: In My Own Words* (Liguori, MO: Liguori, 1989), 33.

53. Mother Teresa, *Thirsting for God,* 194.

54. Mother Teresa, *Thirsting for God,* 195.

55. Spink, 70.

56. Gonzalez-Balado, *Mother Teresa*, 63.

57. Mother Teresa, *One Heart Full of Love*, 92.

58. Mother Teresa, *Thirsting for God*, 84.

59. It should also be pointed out that Jesus numbered among his secret followers the Pharisee Nicodemus (John 3:1) and another member of the Sanhedrin, Joseph of Arimathea; both of these influential Jewish men tended to the body of the crucified Christ (John 19:38–42).

60. Mother Teresa, *One Heart Full of Love*, 9.

61. For more information, read John of Hildesheim, *The Three Kings of Cologne: an Early English Translation of the "Historia Trium Regum"* (Henderson, NV: Hard Press, 2012).

62. Mother Teresa, *Thirsting for God*, 12.

63. Adapted from "Prayer for the Intercession of Blessed Mother Teresa of Calcutta," Catholic News Agency, http://www.catholicnewsagency.com/resources/prayers/prayers-to-saints/prayer-for-the-intercession-of-blessed-mother-teresa-of-calcutta/.

64. Paul Murray, *I Loved Jesus in the Night: Teresa of Calcutta, A Secret Revealed* (Brewster, MA: Paraclete, 2008), 53.

65. Chawla, 124.

66. Pius IX, *Ineffabilis Deus*, quoting DS 2803.

67. Mother Teresa, *Thirsting for God*, 190.

68. Mother Teresa, *Thirsting for God*, 143.

69. Edward Le Joly and Jaya Chaliha, *Reaching Out in Love* (New York: Barnes & Noble, 2002), 35.

ABOUT THE AUTHOR

Heidi Hess Saxton is a Catholic editor, wife, and mother, and is author of several books. A convert to the Catholic faith since 1995, Saxton holds a master's in theology from Sacred Heart Major Seminary in Detroit. As part of her undergraduate studies at Bethany College of Missions in Minneapolis, she spent an internship in Senegal that sparked a lifelong interest in missions—an interest that connected her in a very personal way with the life and work of St. Teresa of Calcutta. Heidi is now editorial director of Servant, an imprint of Franciscan Media. She writes for adoptive, foster, and special-needs families at her blog, A Mother on the Road Less Traveled.

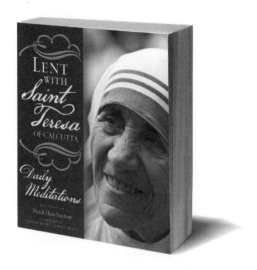

Take your own small steps in the footprints of this spiritual giant
through these Lenten reflection based on the lectionary.
Each day features a meditation from Scripture
and a lesson from the life of St. Teresa.
Learn how this great saint can be your spiritual companion.